How to Day Trade: The Plain Truth

ROSS CAMERON

Published by Warrior Trading, Great Barrington, Massachusetts.

Library of Congress Cataloging-in-Publication Data is Available:

ISBN number 979-8-218-21697-9

Cover Design: ThinkFast LLC

Important Notes

Ross Cameron's experience with trading is not typical. Becoming an experienced trader takes hard work, dedication, and a significant amount of time.

Your results may differ materially from those expressed by Warrior Trading due to a number of factors. We do not track the typical results of our past or current customers. As a provider of educational courses, we do not have access to the personal trading accounts or brokerage statements of our customers. As a result, we have no reason to believe our customers perform better or worse than traders as a whole.

Available research data suggests that most day traders are NOT profitable.

In a research paper published in 2014 titled "Do Day Traders Rationally Learn About Their Ability?", professors from the University of California studied 3.7 billion trades from the Taiwan Stock Exchange between 1992-2006 and found that only 9.81% of day trading volume was generated by predictably profitable traders and that these predictably profitable traders constitute less than 3% of all day traders on an average day.

In a 2005 article published in the Journal of Applied Finance titled "The Profitability of Active Stock Traders," professors at the University of Oxford and the University College Dublin found that out of 1,146 brokerage accounts day trading the US markets between March 8, 2000 and June 13, 2000, only 50% were profitable with an average net profit of $16,619.

In a 2003 article published in the Financial Analysts Journal titled "The Profitability of Day Traders," professors at the University of Texas found that out of 334 brokerage accounts day trading the US markets between February 1998 and October 1999, only 35% were profitable and only 14% generated profits in excess of $10,000.

The range of results in these three studies exemplify the challenge of determining a definitive success rate for day traders. At a minimum, these studies indicate at least 50% of aspiring day traders will not be profitable. This reiterates that consistently making money trading stocks is not easy. Day trading is a high risk activity and can result in the loss of your entire investment. Any trade or investment is at your own risk.

All information discussed is for educational and informational purposes only and should not be considered tax, legal or investment advice. A reference to a stock is not an indication to buy or sell that stock or commodity.

This does not represent our full disclaimer. Please read our complete disclaimer here: www.warriortrading.com/disclaimer/

Citations for Disclaimer

Barber, Brad & Lee, Yong-Ill & Liu, Yu-Jane & Odean, Terrance. (2014). Do Day Traders Rationally Learn About Their Ability?. SSRN Electronic Journal. https://papers.ssrn.com/sol3/papers.cfm?abstract_id=2535636

Garvey, Ryan and Murphy, Anthony, The Profitability of Active Stock Traders. Journal of Applied Finance , Vol. 15, No. 2, Fall/Winter 2005. Available at SSRN: https://ssrn.com/abstract=908615

Douglas J. Jordan & J. David Diltz (2003) The Profitability of Day Traders, Financial Analysts Journal, 59:6, 85-94, DOI: https://www.tandfonline.com/doi/abs/10.2469/faj.v59.n6.2578

If you have dreamed of becoming a day trader, this book
is dedicated to you. You and I are so much alike.
We share the same dream and I hope we have the same drive.
I'm just a little farther down the path than you. I'm here to
support you, and I hope this book is a way of sending the
ladder back down to help you in your journey.

Table of Contents

CHAPTER 1

The Myth and the Reality

THIS BOOK IS ABOUT DAY TRADING, but of course you already knew that from the cover. I bring it up because that is where the similarities end between this book and all the others I've seen about day trading. Same topic, but vastly different messages.

How is this book so different?

I *will not* try to convince you that day trading is your ticket to great wealth. In fact, if your personality and circumstances are not suited to day trading, **I'll convince you to stay away from it,** thus saving you all kinds of time, money, and frustration.

This book *is not* a thinly disguised sales pitch to get you into ev-er-more-expensive training and coaching programs. Let's say you think you might be suited for day trading: you can **take the specific steps you learn here, and start your journey** without ever getting additional materials from me.

I *will never* tell you I've "cracked the code" and have **the only true system** for making day trading "easy." Quite the opposite: I'll describe how very hard it is to become a good day trader. You'll see from my audited brokerage statements how I've become reasonably good at it, but also how I'm far from perfect.

You'll discover that I have developed *one approach* to trading, and I make no claims of superiority over other strategies. Other traders may teach very different strategies from mine. That's fine—there is no single solution to most challenges in life, and day trading is no different.

Everyone has an opinion

In my more than a decade of being in this business, I've been to a lot of social gatherings and events where the ice-breaker is usually the good old "What do you do?"

I dread when people ask me that, because if I choose to tell them I'm a day trader, I can count on a strong reaction. Usually not an en-thusiastic, positive one. After all, if you follow the financial markets and media at all, you can't help but hear about a few so-called day traders who decided to dabble in some hot stock and soon are bragging on social media about how they're up a million dollars and will be retiring before the age of 30.

Or you might hear about the guy—it's usually a guy—who made some money on a tip, felt like he now had a hot hand, and sunk his savings into a stock. He was assured by *both* the gurus on X or Reddit and the TV-network loudmouths that this stock was the "next Tesla" and it would be "going places" very soon. Except with no strategy for managing risk, when the stock reversed, his account followed, and he became another statistic of a failed trader.

Some people experience big winners on beginner's luck, and others lose it all in risky gambles. A few professional traders survive the ups and downs of the market and maintain long track records of consistency. For them, it's an uphill battle to explain how professional day trading bears little resemblance to public opinion.

Day trading sure has a reputation.

Why this book

I wrote this book to bring real-world clarity to that sensationalized reputation surrounding day trading. You are going to see throughout this book that I will be very blunt with you, and here's the first instance: Day trading is like a magnet that strongly attracts some people and strongly repels others. The problem is that it often attracts the wrong people, and drives away other folks who might be great at it, if they only knew the facts. I will fix that in these pages.

> "Day trading is like a magnet that strongly attracts some people and strongly repels others. The problem is that it often attracts the wrong people, and drives away other folks who might be great at it, if they only knew the facts. I will fix that in these pages."

I have the following goals for this book:

1. I must show that **I know what I'm talking about** when it comes to day trading. You'll see that the profession did not come easily for me, but that I've been reasonably successful at it.

2. I will **blow up the many myths**

and misconceptions that form a hard shell around day trading. It's difficult to think of other professions that are as misunderstood, though I'm sure there are some.

3. I'll **paint a realistic picture of what day trading is and is not,** from someone who's not afraid to show you the good, the bad, and the ugly.

    As best I can in book form, I'll give you a sense of **what it's like to sit at a computer and trade stocks like a pro,** but also how it will work when you're a beginner. (Spoiler alert: The main action happens *between your ears*.) You will get a clear sense of whether this profession is a good fit with your personality or not.

4. I'll provide a **detailed and realistic step-by-step path** of how you could dip your toe into this business, and then maybe your foot. There is the wrong way to get started that causes most people to fail, and then there is at least one right way. I'll cover them both.

    Another spoiler alert: You'll not get any "magic keys" to day trading in this book, or "secrets that the big guys don't want you to know." That's the clickbait that attracts the wrong crowd.

"A trusted friend"

I've written this book with a certain image of you and myself in my mind: I imagine that we met some years ago, and have had lots of great conversations. We've been through enough so that we can dispense with dancing around a topic. In other words, we talk straight with each other.

You know that I've made a living by day trading. For a while you shrugged and thought: *Hey, whatever. Not my cup of tea, but to each his own.*

But maybe your circumstances changed. Maybe COVID forced you to work from home, and now your boss is forcing you to go back into the office. Maybe you heard about crypto traders or about the crazy-meteoric rise of stocks like GameStop. (It went from $19 to $483 in 24 days.[1]) Or maybe you and I were catching up one day, and you decided to ask me in more detail about this day trading thing I do.

---

[1] https://www.empirestatetribune.com/est/2/17/2021/6imbc9tmazrk2mupt57xphu5lblexa

For my part, I've not volunteered much about my profession because I value our friendship and figure that you're as misinformed about day trading as the next person. I don't feel like explaining the realities of my career if you're not interested, beyond being polite about "how's it going" on any given day.

I think of this book as our conversations that happened once you sat up and asked me in earnest about the crazy line of work I'm in, whether it was possible to "make a fast fortune" the way people brag on social media, and a hundred other questions.

Because I value our relationship, I'm not going to sugar-coat my answers. I will not tell you what you want to hear. I will not try to convince you of anything, but I'll try to give you a brutally honest brain dump of all the good and bad bits.

Let's say you're not cut out for day trading. It would be great if you find that out just by reading this book, because I'll have saved you a ton of money and headaches versus learning the hard way.

Then again, let's say you have always thought that day trading was for people with more money than brains. Then you discover from this book that in fact, the *real* profession is nothing of the sort, and it meshes nicely with your personality. That's an even better outcome.

Providing solid, experience-based information is what this book is about. You say you have a bunch of questions for me and you want those straight answers? Let's get into it.

CHAPTER 2

Who am I to Talk about Day Trading?

THE INVESTING WORLD IS INHABITED BY ALL KINDS OF PEOPLE. You have those who lost a bunch of money and don't want to talk about it. A number of people have made money and have no desire to discuss it, either because they're too busy making money or they think the more they blab, the greater the competition.

Let's narrow the focus to just those people who are willing to give you information or their opinions about investing, and further narrow it to day trading specifically. These people fall into several groups:

They've never day traded, but they "know a guy." That guy may have lost his life savings, or maybe he did really well. In either case, the advice is based on second-hand information, and probably partial information at that. Was it really "day trading" or did the guy buy a stock based on a hot tip, and months later he sold it? That's not day trading. If you're a real day trader, you buy and sell on the same day. You do not carry any positions over to the next day.

Another group of people dabbled in day trading themselves, but not by first learning any strategies. Brokerage firms make that really easy to do, assuming you have the minimum amount of money to start with and basic computer equipment. (Much more on that later.)

People who do this sort of dabbling can sometimes win, and usually get their butts handed to them. Advice and information from these types of people is going to be incomplete and inconsistent.

Some people have tried day trading, were serious for a while, then got burned. They did not have a support system to help them to figure out what went wrong, and how to adjust their trading strategies. These traders will share with you their horror stories, but may not understand the root cause of their own failures. Though they provide a tale of caution, they may be unable to communicate the strategies or mental processes that lead to success.

Other people have done day trading and are quite visible online. They might have courses or channels and charge for their services. The only problem is they only make their money on courses and are not profitable traders. They'll be happy to talk about their wins, but will not share their brokerage statements.

Then there's the largest group of people. They are happy to dispense opinions to you, but it's only based on what they've heard about day trading through the news media, social media, or the movies.

Do you see a trend here? These people do not have substantial personal experience based on putting in the hard work to learn proven strategies, and then trade over a long period.

The six criteria for a good teacher

Let me put it another way: you should only learn day trading from someone who:
1. Has personally done it
2. Has traded over not just days or weeks, but years
3. Has been *consistently* successful at it
4. Will share with you not just the successes, but also the challenges and downright failures; and
5. Can document that track record. By "document" I don't mean the occasional tweet of the guy standing in front of his rented Ferrari. I mean audited brokerage statements that cover all of that person's trading activity.
6. Finally, he or she is willing to teach you.

No one maintains a list of people who meet all these criteria. I'm sure several people meet some criteria, and maybe a handful who publish audited brokerage statements.

Because you took the time to pick up this book and read it, you deserve to know how I stack up to those criteria:
1. I've personally traded.
2. I have done so full-time for more than a decade.
3. In terms of consistency, my accuracy rate is 69 percent. (Accuracy is the percent of all trades that made money.)
4. My YouTube channel has more than a million subscribers and over ten years of educational videos. I routinely upload

recaps of my trading where I highlight both my winners and my losers.

5. I pride myself on transparency. That's why on my website you can see my audited brokerage statements going back for years. This audit verifies over $10 million in trading profits.[2]

6. I enjoy teaching and am willing to teach you.

7. I'm going to add a seventh, bonus criterion: I didn't have an easy time becoming a disciplined, successful trader. Far from it, as you'll see in this chapter. I think this may be an important factor, because some prodigy who seems naturally suited to a profession may not be the best person for the rest of us to learn from.

"But Ross, if you're so successful at day trading, why on earth would you be teaching? Isn't it true that 'those who can't do something, teach it'?"

We're getting right into the no-nonsense questions, aren't we? Good. I get that question all the time, and it's a reasonable one to ask. Here is a multi-part answer:

I'm pretty sure that teaching is in my DNA. My grandmothers were teachers on both my mom and dad's side. My grandfather worked at Dartmouth College, my uncle is a professor at Yale, and my mom was an "activity therapist" or type of teacher at a nearby hospital. From an early age, I was accustomed to being around people who enjoyed teaching. I also was a big brother, which meant I was always a bit of a teacher to my sister. I simply like to teach. Long before I was into day trading, I taught ceramics classes in Vermont. Later, when I was a trading cub, I gravitated to moderating a trading chat forum. I didn't know a ton about trading, but I could answer beginners' questions and that's what I did—for free.

More than ten years ago I shrugged and decided to do videos while I traded and then talk about the trades on camera. I made zero money for quite a while, but that was not the point, because it helped my thought process to describe my trades out loud. I also found that viewers would hold my feet to the fire, so to speak, with their comments.

Besides, as you will come to find out in these pages, there is no

---

[2] Reminder, although my results are not typical, they are real. You can see my audited performance here: https://www.warriortrading.com/ross-camerons-verified-day-trading-earnings/

reason for me to hold back. There are no "secrets" in real day trading. No silver bullets that give you an edge. As you will see, it's about dedicating yourself to learning a great deal about how markets move and how other investors think.

"That's cool that you like to teach, Ross. Why don't you continue teaching and simply give it away for free? Why do you charge for it?"

Another good question. I do give a great deal away for free, in the form of my continuous flow of YouTube videos, and some materials on my website. Why don't I give it all away? Because I can't. I decided early on that in order to provide my community with the best possible experience, I would need to combine all the must-have trading tools into one platform. I hired a development team and built a custom platform for day traders. This platform provides useful information to traders through its stock scanners, stock charts, chat rooms, and live broadcasts.

As you can imagine, it costs money every day the platform is online and running. I have no qualms about charging a fair price for a platform that makes it easier for the average trader to find strong stocks and actionable trade ideas.

Back to my story

I was born in Brattleboro, Vermont, in 1985. My mom worked in the Brattleboro school system before getting a job at the Brattleboro Retreat (the hospital I mentioned earlier). She worked there for 41 years before being unceremoniously laid off. My dad worked at the Brattleboro Retreat as well in the building maintenance department. He had been a Fulbright Scholar but had a variety of health issues in his life that greatly affected him, and also who I grew up to become.

My mom wanted to make sure that I got into the habit of working from a young age. She was sort of my agent, helping me to get a paper route, and then jobs like mowing lawns and maintaining swimming pools.

Pivotal moment

I was at a Montessori school during seventh and eighth grade. My teacher Kevin did an amazing semester on the stock market, where he had us pair up. My buddy Cooper and I created a dummy portfolio and each day we'd chart the prices in class and discuss the stocks.

This got me a little inspired, and I think it showed. Another project at the school was to pair up with someone and write biographies of each other. My friend took this photo of me and wrote on the back: "20 years from now, Ross will be living in New York City and working on Wall Street."

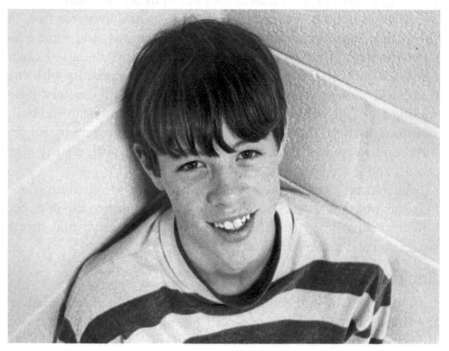

Figure 2-1: Future day trader

The portfolio we created intrigued me, so I called up my local Edward Jones office. I told them I wanted to buy shares of American Ski Company. It was trading around 90 cents then. The broker said: "Okay, how much do you want to invest?"

"I have $100."

He said: "Well that's going to be a problem. We charge a commission of $50 to buy and another $50 to sell."

"Oh. Never mind."

The stock market went on the back burner and I found a new interest in the computer lab at school.

I started a business with my neighbor to build websites for different businesses in Brattleboro. That's when I learned how to code in

HTML, and also a little graphic design. I enjoyed the feeling of being in business for myself. I continued building websites for myself and for friends over the years, including the first website at Warrior Trading, but web design didn't become a continuing business for me.

After a while, I developed an interest in architecture and also ceramics. In high school and during college I taught classes in ceramics to adults and kids at a local studio.

Coolest kid ever

While in high school, I had another friend named Ben. Get this: as a high school kid, Ben made $16,000 by trading a penny stock. It wasn't day trading; Ben had been given a tip by someone's dad and he acted on it.

Ben then proceeded to buy a used Nissan Pathfinder and outfit his basement with an awesome sound system, jukebox, and an arcade machine. This all made a **big** impression on me! I'm like: *If Ben can do it, maybe so can I.*

Ben didn't continue to invest—he blew that money pretty quickly— but it got me thinking. I opened an Ameritrade account in the summer of 2001 and funded it with my life savings from mowing and such, which amounted to about $1,000. I bought a few shares of ExxonMobil, Caterpillar, Cannondale Bicycle, and American Ski Company.

By the end of the summer, my portfolio was basically unchanged, to my chagrin. I didn't have quite the hot hand that Ben did.

As I made my way through high school, I put little thought into college and did not study for the SAT exams. I had become a very anxious teenager, and the prospect of going to college overwhelmed me to the point of paralysis. But my mom urged me to apply to schools anyway, and I got accepted to Colby-Sawyer College in New Hampshire with an art scholarship.

I studied art and education with an eye to maybe becoming an art teacher. That would allow me to do ceramics, and I'd have a teaching certificate to fall back on and I could become a regular teacher, if necessary.

Downturn

That was the plan, at least. What got in the way were my panic attacks. They began in high school and got worse in college. They were bad enough that I dropped out of college after three semesters.

My anxiety was made worse when my father was diagnosed with stage-four lung cancer and given one year to live in 2005. As a college dropout, I was living back at home in Vermont to help in any way that I could. My mom, working again as my agent, helped find me a job pumping gas at the local Sunoco station.

This was a pretty tough period for me, not only because of my father's situation and my anxiety attacks, but also because I felt like I was going nowhere. There wasn't a lot of ambition in the folks I hung around with at the gas station.

I thought that what might work for my situation was to run some kind of business, like maybe the ceramics studio I had worked at for a while. That might be a way to make a living more on my own terms. I began to think I just needed to make enough money to buy a piece of land and build a cabin with a ceramics studio. I envisioned a life living off the grid, selling my work at summer craft fairs and festivals, and teaching as needed. However, with a lack of funds to make that dream happen, and with the guilt of having only partially finished my degree, I decided to go back to college in Vermont.

While my father was sick, I attended classes at the Community College of Vermont in Brattleboro. After my father passed away, I enrolled at Vermont College, which had an online program. Basically a semester involved reading fifteen books and then writing a ten-page paper on each one of them. I did that for three semesters and got my four-year degree.

Part of the subject of all those books I was reading involved architecture. I'd focused on mid-century modern, American modern, and European modern styles, with a helping of urban planning thrown in. I chose to study architecture not because it was necessarily more interesting than ceramics, but because I thought it was much easier to read and write about.

Big city

While I was living at home and finishing my degree, I continued working in the ceramics studio, but the hours were limited and I wasn't saving any money. At the time, I had a girlfriend from Vermont who was living in New York City while she was going to school. I took the train down to visit her, and what started as a long weekend turned into my living in New York City with her for the next four years.

I needed a job and applied for two internships. The first was at a hedge fund. In characteristic Wall Street parlance, they told me to fuck off. They said my degree was not even close to being relevant.

The other internship I applied for was at an architecture studio, and I got that job. It was with a small firm, which meant that I ended up doing a lot of different things there. I managed a construction budget, worked on their website, visited contractors, invoiced clients, helped get permits from the building department, and so on.

I worked there for several years and eventually thought that maybe I could start a business of my own along the same lines. Around this time, I felt a pull back to Vermont. I'd go back there on some weekends, and the contrast was sharp between the pressure of Manhattan and the rolling hills of Vermont.

This was also a difficult time because the panic attacks increased. It didn't help that my boss, the studio owner, was your classic New York jerk: super rude to people, super entitled, and a screamer. Monday mornings often began with this guy yelling at his wife, his employees, and his contractors.

By this point, my girlfriend was tired of living in the city and decided to move back to Vermont. It was hard enough to make ends meet in the city and if she left, I'd have the entire rent on my shoulders.

We both moved back to Vermont, and I continued to work at the architecture studio, but remotely. After a bit, my girlfriend and I parted ways, and I was living back at my mom's house, now in my mid-20s.

In 2009, when my sister turned 21, we each got $100,000 from my dad's estate. That money had come from when he and my uncle sold their mother's house in New Hampshire in the early 1990s. I wanted to invest at least part of that money. The problem was that, aside from Ben's cool 16 grand and my limited experience with large-cap stocks, I didn't know how to invest.

I moved into a small farmhouse not far from my childhood home, and got reacquainted with a girl I'd known in high school. About a year later, we got married.

The New York job remained stressful in terms of interacting with my boss. After one of his bigger outbursts at me over the phone, I quit on the spot. I was now unemployed.

I had already been focused on investing the money my father left me but I was using a financial adviser. The results were far from impressive and, despite the poor performance, I was still paying fees to the adviser. I thought maybe I could do better than the investment results I'd seen so far. The good news was I had some money available. The bad news was I had no idea how to manage that money, especially given my new "job status."

Backing into a decision

I had some thinking to do. I was only 24, and I had $100 grand. If I played my cards right, it seemed like that would go a long way toward a good retirement nest egg.

Could I maybe put it in nice, safe investments that paid dividends and would not blow up? The recent subprime-mortgage crisis put a huge dent in the American economy, and I needed secure investments.

Hmmm. A dividend of 2.5 percent on that entire $100 grand would equal $2,500 per year, gross. That was a non-starter.

When I was living in New York City, I'd been making $45,000 per year. The costs of living were so much higher there than in Vermont. I figured that if I could gross $1,000 a week, that would be a pretty good living.

Okay, so $1,000 a week meant $50,000 a year in round numbers. I've got $100,000 to do it with. What am I going to do in order to get there?

I might find junk bonds that paid fifteen percent or maybe eighteen percent. That would get me part of the way there, but nothing would return fifty percent!

I thought about my friend Ben. As a mere kid, he scored that $16,000 in the penny stock market. I didn't know what he started out with, but it was probably less than five grand. He was able to triple or quadruple it in short order.

Hmmm again: If I could start with that amount and do a Ben-type of trade just three lousy times in a whole year, that'd be 45 grand! And I knew a whole lot more about trading now than Ben had known. That seemed like what I logically needed to do in order to turn that inheritance into something sustainable.

In hindsight, working backwards like that is the worst thing you can do as a foundation for day trading. You should want to explore trading through genuine curiosity about learning it, and not from the pressure of putting food on the table.

It felt like a tremendous amount of pressure on me, but it also seemed like a prudent calculation at the time. I was fine with staying home and learning everything I could about trading, but that was not my wife's idea of fun. She wanted to travel and she did not scrimp and save.

A penny here, a penny there

To follow in Ben's footsteps, I began my new endeavor by Googling "penny stocks." There were plenty of websites dedicated to hot penny stocks. Talk about hype: everywhere I looked, I was told about stocks "set to take off" or that were rated as "strong buys." Stocks that would "disrupt the trillion-dollar sports industry" or that were "wildly undervalued."

What pretty much all of them did was tempt you to put in your email address or cell phone number, promising free alerts for the next big mover. Many of them had countdown clocks on their sites, showing when that next amazing tip would drop—if you were signed up to get it.

Once you signed up, two things were likely to happen: First, you'd get a steady stream of "hot tips" that the website was paid to promote. Second, they'd sell your contact information to many other services. In no time at all, my inbox was flooded with "hot penny stock" alerts.

I signed up at a lot of these sites, plus joined some forums and message boards. Like most things on the internet, a few were well done with useful information, and most of it was useless. It didn't take long to see which was which.

Eventually I settled on a handful of sources for stock information, and I actually had a little beginner's luck. I'd get the email alert, buy a stock, and I'd sell it for a small profit. With other tips, I lost money.

It also didn't take long for me to get frustrated. First, I felt like I was 100 percent dependent on waiting for the next alert. Then when I got it, I'd have to act *immediately* on it, or I'd feel like I missed some of the action.

The second frustration was with some of the "premium" alert services I joined. They seemed to be run by successful investors, and they reliably sent email and text alerts for the trades that the head of the service was taking. They might even provide a "watch list" of stocks.

But the problem was that there was this huge disconnect between their results with the stocks they traded, and a beginner trader like me developing a process for actually finding *which exact stocks to trade.*

How did they find the stock? Why did they get in? At what price did they get in? It was especially frustrating when there was no news about the stock, but it was a purely technical reason for the recommendation. What I soon realized is that these services wouldn't teach you to develop your own strategy, because it would be bad for their business model. As soon as you became independent, you wouldn't need them anymore. So they kept you guessing when it came to finding stocks to trade.

They were handing me a fish, in the form of a buy alert, but they were not teaching me to fish. I clearly had a lot of learning ahead of me.

Initially I put about $5,000 into an E*TRADE account, but almost immediately I got what's known as a PDT notification.

> "...there was this huge disconnect between their results with the stocks they traded, and a beginner trader like me developing a process for actually finding which exact stocks to trade."

The Pattern Day Trader (PDT) rule is a designation from the Securities and Exchange Commission that applies to traders who make four or more day trades in their margin account over a five business-day period.

A day trade is when you purchase or short a security and then sell or cover the same security in the same day. Much more on this later.

The bottom line was that with my $5,000 account, I could only make three day trades in any rolling five-day period. If I raised my account value above $25,000, the restriction no longer applied. So that's what I did.

In my first year of trading, I made around $30,000. On the one hand, I came up short against my $50k goal, but I felt pretty good about the year because it was a proof of concept that day trading could work for me. It was my first year of dedicated trading, and I was green!

(If a trader makes money or loses money in a day, it's a "green day" or "red day." The same is true for red weeks, green years, and so on.)

I felt like I was close to turning the corner. *This will just keep getting a little bit better*, I thought.

Only it didn't. In my second year, I lost everything that I had made in the first year. On the one hand, I was breakeven after two years. Not terrible. But as I went into my third year, I continued on the trend of having small green days and large red days.

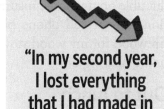

"In my second year, I lost everything that I had made in the first year."

So far, I was red in my endeavor to be a trader.

To make matters worse, I had spent the profit in the first year on my cost of living, and my continued expenses each month in year two and year three were eating away at my trading account balance.

My account was down to the minimum required to day trade of $25,000. It would frequently dip below $25,000 and I'd have to add a little money to get back above $25,000 so I could keep trading.

I also had accumulated credit card debt just to pay for living expenses. It was the one-off expenses that kept adding up. I put my dog's emergency vet bill on one card, a repair of my car on another, and the trip to a friend's wedding on yet another card. I charged these expenses so I wouldn't have to take cash out of my trading account, but I kept falling further behind and interest rates didn't help.

It wasn't like I had taken that $100,000 and blown it on man-cave toys; I had been careful with the money. Still, I felt like an idiot, a failure, and a disappointment to my father. All I had left of his money was the $25,000 trading account.

Double-barrel emotions

There I was, the guy with the regular anxiety attacks, and to that I added regular bouts of guilt at losing most of my dad's inheritance. I was in year three with five credit cards each maxed out to nearly $30,000 in total debt, and a $25,000 trading account that I couldn't seem to grow.

I felt like I was up against the ropes. I was deeply engaged in trading and wanted to extend my knowledge and turn that corner, but at the current rate, I was going to run out of runway before taking off.

That's when I thought seriously about getting a job, like working the 3-11pm shift at a ski area with my friend David. I also thought about every way to lighten my expense load: I could increase the deductible on my home insurance, and downgrade or eliminate subscriptions to our cell phone plan and Netflix. I had no problem cutting firewood for my wood stove, so I wouldn't have to buy another tank of home heating oil.

Out to lunch

I had gotten myself into this financial bind. I had not only invested in stocks, but I'd invested in myself in the form of knowledge about how to trade. I was willing to work hard to turn that corner. I was also willing to tighten my belt financially and buy more runway so I could finally reap the rewards, but my wife was not on board. She wanted a husband who could take care of her without needing to cut back on spending. She didn't want to choose between taking a vacation or having a few more months to focus on getting a new endeavor off the ground.

"Why don't you get a real job?"

"Why don't you get a real job? All my friends from New Hampshire are *real men*, unlike YOU. They work in construction. They're painters and electricians. And look at you. You're trying to make money in the stock market! What do you have to show for it? You're a loser."

Following the Great Recession of 2007-2009, many people had a deep loathing for the big Wall Street banks that brought the financial system to its knees. I think she fell into the belief system that Wall Street and big banks were evil. It wasn't that I disagreed, but I was the little guy, trying to make a little money off Wall Street while living in my farmhouse in Vermont.

In any case, not long after that "conversation," she said, "I'm going to lunch with some friends." I was like, "Okay, see you later. I'll be here, studying my charts."

Except I didn't see her later. She never came back. All her stuff was in the house as if she was going to lunch, except she never came back.

The first day, I thought something terrible might have happened. I had no idea what was going on. This was crazy. Then we spoke, and she said plans changed and she was with friends and would be home later. Except she didn't come home later. I'm like: *Maybe she needs time to unwind and cool down. After all, our situation isn't that bad compared to other people.* But she never came back. Three weeks of this passed, so I called her. "I don't know what to do, but I do know that this is crazy. If you don't come back by the end of this week, I'm going to file for a divorce."

She didn't come back.

That was actually probably a good thing. She wanted to live a lifestyle that I couldn't provide. She wanted me to work her idea of a "regular job" that I didn't want. And she wasn't willing to get a job herself.

After turning that page, I doubled down on reducing my expenses, because it was now just me and my dog. I cut firewood and also cut every expense I could think of. I made Craigslist ads for stuff in my barn—stuff that I didn't really need. Through all of this, I was able to buy myself some time and extend that runway.

Wanted: guru

Now that I was back on my own, I could really take immersion learning to another level. I continued to look for sources of information on not just *what* to buy, but *why* it's a good buy, and *when* to buy it.

> **"...I doubled down on reducing my expenses, because it was now just me and my dog."**

I found some well-regarded services, but they usually gave advice about mid-cap or large-cap stocks. (I'll explain about mid caps and large caps later, or you can look them up in the glossary if you want to know right now.)

The other issue is these sources might even explain why they liked the stock, and why now was the right time to get into it—but it was a swing trade and not day trade. A "swing trade" is where you hold a stock for days or weeks, versus day trading where you don't hold any stocks overnight.

I could not take that kind of risk. If I held a stock overnight, there could be news about a "secondary offering" or other big event, such that the stock could literally drop 40 or 50 percent overnight. There was no way I could take that kind of risk.

I discovered another source of information, colloquially known as a "squawk box." In the old days this was a type of public-address system in brokerage houses, tied to Wall Street information sources. It later morphed into online chat systems among institutional traders. (Institutions are places like pension funds, big banks, and brokerage houses doing their own trading, or trading on behalf of big clients.)

The squawk box chatter was stuff like, "My source at Goldman told me they're looking to unload a big position on $AAPL (Apple)" or "takeover talk on Alibaba." It might even be something absurdly cryptic like "AAPL+++." Maybe it meant something to a guy in suspenders, chomping on his fat cigar at the Morgan Stanley trading desk, but it had zero value to me in terms of what I could buy with that supposedly hot information.

In the course of all this searching, I began to focus more on traders that were day trading small-cap stocks. I learned about the tools they used, like "gap scanners" and "high of day momentum scanners." (More on these later.)

I never did find someone who was a real mentor to me when I was getting into the business. Instead, it was a slow process of looking around at what was on the internet, and signing up for a lot of mostly free services. Pretty soon I had a firehose of information pouring into my email and phone from all sorts of services that bought and sold my contact information. I deleted most of them and tried a few.

This must have been what prospectors felt and did during the gold rush: you hear some people found gold. Suddenly there's no shortage of tips about "sure things." You know most of them will literally not pan out, but some might! How much of your time and money do you spend chasing these leads? How much do you invest in tools like prospecting gear—or in my case, software to locate those next pockets of gold?

Two steps forward

I continued to trade and learn. I had periods where I traded well and would make a little money. Then I would give it back, and then make money again. It was the classic "two steps forward then two or three steps back." Every six to eight weeks, I'd think: *Oh man, here we go again.*

I might make around $1,000 a week for a nice, consistent run of eight weeks—and then I'd give it all back in a $10,000 loss. Many times those trades were impulsive losses that spiraled quickly into what I called "snowball days." Then I'd have to regroup, get back on the horse, and rebuild again.

> "I felt completely defeated. I walked outside, sat on a stump in the woodshed, and put my head in my hands. What was I going to do?"

The next crisis came when I took around a $5,000 loss in the beginning of a new month. It was August, summer was almost over, and that loss dropped my account down from over $25,000 to about $19,500. I wasn't going to be able to day trade in that account until I funded it with more money, to get it back above $25,000.

My account was offline.

I felt completely defeated. I walked outside, sat on a stump in the woodshed, and put my head in my hands. What was I going to do?

I needed a game plan. No—I needed a *trading plan.* And I also needed $5,000.

Down to my last idea

I had been trying to absorb good ideas from other traders in the online communities I hung out in. During the time my account was offline, I had time to think. One thing I believe I've always been good at is figuring stuff out, instead of just throwing the whole thing out the window. I enjoyed video games growing up and Sudoku puzzles when I was older. Trading seemed like a real-life puzzle. I was at a roadblock on solving this puzzle, but I wasn't ready to give up. Not even close.

I had an Excel spreadsheet of pretty much all of my trades. Part of the reason I kept these detailed notes was because of the relationship I had with the money my dad left me. I felt like I needed to account for every gain and loss, if only to myself.

The information consisted of things like trade date, amount, the stock, how much I made or lost, what was the pattern I saw when I made the trade, and overall comments.

One useful perspective that jumped out at me was to look at the components of my overall performance. True, I had given back my first year's gains in the second year. But I had made *tens of thousands of dollars in gains,* which were offset by a similar amount of losses. My trading had indeed been working well—at times.

Just as traders study the movement of a stock in order to see patterns, I studied my own trades. By this point, I had lots of data in the form of those positive and negative trades. *What was I doing differently when I made money, from when I lost it? It can't be random. What was the pattern? What did the winners have in common?*

I discovered five common denominators. First, I realized I had performed the best on stocks that were up over 10 percent on the day versus the previous day's closing price. For example, a stock priced at $8.00 yesterday was trading at $8.80 or higher today.

Second, the stocks I did the best on always had high volume relative to how many shares usually traded in a single day. This is called *relative volume,* and it's measured as a ratio of today's volume versus what is average for that stock. A stock that had 10 million shares of volume today, but typically trades only 1 million shares of volume per day, is trading with a relative volume of 10.

> "What was I doing differently when I made money, from when I lost it? It can't be random. What was the pattern? What did the winners have in common?"

Third, on higher priced stocks (above $20 per share), I had outsized losses. I would have winners too, but overall I was losing more than I was making on higher priced stocks. I attributed this to the larger ranges higher priced stocks trade in, and how easy it was to take a quick loss that far exceeded my anticipated max loss on the trade. By eliminating stocks priced over $20, and focusing primarily on stocks between $2 and $10—but certainly not more than $20—my historical data showed I would have been more profitable.

Fourth, often the volume and volatility was the result of some type of news about the company. Focusing on stocks with news seemed to eliminate a lot of the false breakouts and unnecessary losses. However, there were times a stock could make big moves due simply to a "technical breakout" or a "short squeeze" where the stock performed outside of expected parameters and traders took notice.

I decided that focusing on stocks with news would be better, but eventually I might be able to trade stocks without news if they proved they were strong.

Fifth, I realized the stocks most likely to go up not just 10 percent, but 30 percent or even 50 percent or more in a day typically had a very limited number of shares available to trade. This is called the *float*, and lower float stocks are more volatile than ones with a higher float.

When a company does an initial public offering (IPO), it sells a fixed number of shares onto the market. Following an IPO, a company can do secondary offerings to sell more shares; this is a form of dilution and generally reduces the stock price. Companies can also conduct share buybacks or reverse splits. Both effectively reduce the number of shares available to trade.

As an example, when GameStop made its meteoric rise, it already had sold about 69 million shares onto the open market. This represented the float of the company. On the days when the stock traded 100 million shares of volume during January 2021, there was so much demand that as soon as somebody sold shares, another person was ready to buy them. With limited supply and massive demand, the stock price continued to surge higher. It is unlikely this would have happened if the float on the stock had been as large as say, Bank of America, with an 8 billion share float.

As it turned out, the first four discoveries—10 percent change on the day; high relative volume; breaking news; and price between $2 and $20—were all based on the criteria that create a high level of demand. The fifth is based on supply. High demand and limited supply creates an imbalance, which leads to momentum and volatility. This is what real day traders are looking for. I can't believe it took me this long to figure it out. It all comes back to supply and demand.

Up to this point I had tried a little of everything. I had traded stocks like Apple. My thought at the time had been that it was a good idea to get to know one stock really well, so why not take an iconic stock like Apple, which after all had made a fortune for many investors before me.

I had tried trading options, which have the benefit of settling overnight and requiring less buying power. Unfortunately they were really only profitable in the rare occasions that the underlying asset made a very large move. This was too inconsistent to be my bread and butter strategy. I tried penny stocks, but unlike my friend Ben, I found the losses were much larger than the gains. Penny stocks weren't a consistent way for me to make money, and they forced me to be 100 percent dependent on trade alerts.

I also tried small caps. Small caps are relatively smaller companies, as we'll discuss in a later chapter. Most stocks under $20 are considered small caps. It turns out that I found success in this area; I just hadn't realized it before, because I had spent my first two and a half years trading a little of everything.

Trading a little of everything can be good early on because you'll discover what strategies match your risk tolerance and personality. Unfortunately, in my case, trading a little of everything *at the same time* and with real money caused real problems. It made it difficult to realize that while I had been losing money overall during my second year, one strategy I'd been trading had quietly been outperforming all the others.

With new insights into my winners and losers, I created a plan for getting back on track. A solution to the puzzle was within reach. I decided to stop trading Apple and other stocks that had super-high ownership by big institutions like mutual funds and pension funds. These stocks rarely had high relative volume and rarely were up over 10 percent in a day.

When trading those stocks, I felt like I was playing chess against a supercomputer. I wasn't wrong: I later learned that most volume in these stocks is actually generated by high-frequency trading algorithms and computers run by institutional trading firms.

Cutting out most large caps meant I could cut out options trading because I only traded options on large caps. I could also eliminate penny stocks because I found I was consistently losing money on stocks under $1.

Based on my self analysis, my best trades were on stocks that were up over 10 percent, had high relative volume, had some type of breaking news, were priced between $2 and $20, and had a float of fewer than 50 million shares. I could more easily see trading patterns on those stocks, but certainly no stock had big days all the time. That meant I was going to need to get comfortable trading different stocks every day, but if I used those five filters, I could quickly get a sense of which ones looked like they *might* have a big day.

Although there will always be some exceptions—such as trading GameStop which was over $20 and with a 69 million share float—when I was at rock bottom, I couldn't afford to deviate from what my metrics were telling me. It was time to check myself into "Trader Rehab" which you'll hear more about later. Though my back was up against the wall, I now was armed with a real trading plan based on my own historical data. This strategy was not based on stock alerts from penny stock newsletters, or from one of the hundreds of trading gurus blasting out texts and emails, but were solid insights based on when I had actually made money from trading.

This is the blueprint I wish somebody had given me when I got started. At least I had it now. Better late than never.

I still needed $5,000 to get my account back up above the $25,000 PDT minimum. A few years earlier I had bought a rare European import Mercedes with a manual transmission and a diesel engine that had been left to rot in my friend's yard. He let me have it for $350 as long as I could get it out of his yard.

"I knew what I needed to do. Now I just had to execute."

I fixed it up with new brakes, calipers, all new suspension, and new paint. During that project I bought a second Mercedes of the same vintage for spare parts. I loved those cars, but I needed the money, and now with a trading plan in place, I felt confident in my decision: I listed the cars for sale and sold them both. My account was back above $25,000.

Now I was *really* up against the ropes. I didn't have much left that I could sell if I had another $5,000 loss.

Discipline

I knew what I needed to do. Now I just had to execute, and that was by no means a trivial task. I was asking myself to change my behavior on a dime.

Trading discipline was something I had struggled with early on. Even before having my new insights, I had known about how trading was an emotional roller coaster, and how there were certain behaviors to avoid. I created these rules to try to prevent blow ups.

Even though I tried to be disciplined, in my first two and a half years of trading, on some days I'd basically break all the rules I'd set for myself:

- I would be green, then I would give back half of my profit and would keep trading;
- I would hold past my max loss on a trade and hope it bounced back;
- I would average down on a trade (adding to a loser);
- I would trade past the maximum daily loss amount I'd previously set as a boundary;
- I'd trade even after having three consecutive losers, a red flag that should have told me to stop;
- I'd revenge trade, where I tried to make up for previous bad trades by jumping prematurely into another;
- I'd then get furious at what just happened to that last trade and would FOMO in long at the very top (FOMO is "fear of missing out" and I'd buy at the top—when the signals told me not to—just in case it was going higher).

In short, I got emotionally hijacked. And I literally would then pay the price. I was bad at walking away when I was having a bad day, and it was costing me a lot of money. This was the reason I'd have eight or ten good weeks in a row, then in one day, give it all back.

"I had come to know one other thing: Successful traders did not trade for ten hours a day."

Now it was different. Now I had no choice but to be disciplined. If I wanted to avoid pumping gas or working the 3-11pm shift at the ski resort, I needed to follow my own rules. I had to go cold turkey on my emotions, set firm guardrails for my trading, strap myself in, and do what I knew.

I had come to know one other thing: successful traders did not trade for ten hours a day. The focus and discipline to be ON—to be watching a stock second by second intently—simply could not be done for ten hours a day. Sure, anyone can sit like a zombie and stare at a monitor for ten hours at a time, but that's not what professional day traders were doing.

I set myself a limit to trade for two hours a day in the morning. Then I would go outside and split wood. After all, I needed to get ready for the winter and I was *not* going to be buying that home heating oil!

After I finished stacking enough wood, I decided to paint the house. It wasn't so much for aesthetic reasons as it was to preserve my house investment. Besides, the farmhouse was white and a few cans of white paint didn't cost that much versus the trading losses it was preventing.

"I developed my mantra:

Get green and shut it down."

I got into a routine, kept myself busy, and I felt very productive. In fact, it almost felt like therapy, because I was in control of my tiny little world: I had my strict time window of trading, during which I followed equally strict rules about that trading. Then I would get off the computer.

To be more clear: I shut off my computer and unplugged it. There was even a period when I would put my computer in the car. Anything to prevent myself from opening that computer again for the day. I knew that people who wanted to watch less TV would take the batteries out of the remote and put them in a drawer in the other room. Similarly, I made it hard to look at stocks once I finished my trading session. I could do more wood splitting, scraping, or painting. What I could not allow myself to do was open that computer again until tomorrow.

I developed my mantra: **Get green and shut it down.** In other words, I could trade in my two-hour window. If I made a profitable trade, according to my new criteria, I was green. Shut it down. If my first or second trades were red—again using my criteria—then I might trade again if I saw the right pattern developing. As soon as I got green, or my two-hour window was over, or I hit one of my rules to stop trading—whichever came first—I shut it down.

Tightrope

My guardrails were so tight that I felt like I wasn't on a highway, or even a narrow trail. I needed to walk a trading tightrope. I could not afford to make many mistakes. But this was what I needed.

There were some days when nothing set up. (That is, nothing matched my previously successful trading pattern or "setup" that I was hunting for.) On another day, if I clearly saw my setup, I would trade it with what was a fairly big size for me.

When I saw it clearly, I was going big. *Get green, and shut it down.* If I didn't see it, I wasn't touching it. This was a major turning point for me.

I had been through a multiyear process of experimentation, journaling, and reflecting on the few things that worked and the many that didn't, before I finally started to turn that corner that I had felt had been near for so long. I'm convinced that one big reason I did eventually turn the corner was I stuck with it long enough.

Lonely as it was, I no longer had someone continuously telling me what an idiot I was to be wasting time on the stock market. I also unsubscribed from all the "hot tip" services that simply created dependency on their next alert. I started to be able to go to my little stretch of stream, to my fishing hole, and patiently wait. Some days I caught nothing, but at least I shut it down after a couple of hours. I also didn't chase up and down the stream, listening to others who claimed that they had hooked the monster fish that got away. Other days I caught a fish, and promptly packed up. I wasn't getting rich, but I was getting green on a decidedly more regular basis.

"It took me over two years of studying, testing, failing, and refining to turn that corner and emerge on the other side with a small but powerful set of trading principles."

Two years of work

It took me over two years of studying, testing, failing, and refining to turn that corner and emerge on the other side with a small but powerful set of trading principles. The first one was what I already mentioned: *get green and shut it down.*

The second one, which allowed me to find that fishing hole and start to be somewhat successful, was to focus on the gap scanner each day. This screen showed me which stocks were set to open the highest relative to where they closed the previous day.

This is super-important to view each day for one simple reason that you'll hear me come back to again and again: you need to watch this scanner because huge numbers of other traders are watching it. Traders flock to the top ten gappers. Elsewhere in this book I'll talk about other popular tools and metrics that many traders focus on.

Think about just this one simple measurement—top gappers. Let's say you're really intrigued with a particular stock, and you want to analyze it in depth before deciding to invest in it.

"The difference is gigantic between what *might* move, what *should* move, and what *has* moved."

Here's one way to do it:
- You scrutinize all the financial filings the company has made with the government.
- You set up a Google Alert so you'll be notified whenever the company issues a press release, social-media post, or YouTube video about some company activity.
- CNBC is always playing in the background near your desk, so you can pick up chatter about the stock.
- You run a bunch of financial ratios and other analyses to get a sense about whether this stock is likely to move soon.
- Perhaps you talk it over with your broker or financial advisor, to see what that person thinks.

You can do all of that heavy lifting to try to predict if and when that stock might start to move up—even just a little bit. Then again, you might be rewarded with a stock that goes nowhere for a long time.

Contrast that with finding out in real time about what *has* jumped up. The difference is gigantic between what *might* move, what *should* move, and what *has* moved.

This brings me to the next key principle I began to follow: I wait for a stock to start to move, and then I jump in. I wait for it to prove itself: not that it'll necessarily be the next Apple, but that today, it has the potential to squeeze up 20-30 percent or more.

"Well that sounds fine, Ross, but aren't you ignoring one key thing? By waiting for the stock to move, aren't you giving up some of the upside?"

You are correct. By waiting to see the biggest gappers, I've theoretically given up some of the upside, because someone else indeed got in at the moment that gap happened.

But I'm totally OK with that. Let's briefly return to the fishing analogy. It's well established that sometimes the fish aren't biting. If I wanted, I could sit at the stream all day, every day, waiting for the fish to get hungry. Or I could pay some kid to sit there, and only run to fetch me when the fish in fact are biting.

I consider it not as lost money, but gained opportunities: instead of investing all my time in watching a handful of stocks in the hope that some will move, with stock scanners I can watch *all stocks* and will see when those gaps actually occur, for whatever reason. I will take that tradeoff every day.

Later I will get into strategies for how long I stay in, what I do if I get out and the stock keeps going up, and other situations.

Back to the gaps: I came to realize that there is a mentality in trading that when something starts to move, everyone wants a piece. There is a bit—or more than a bit—of a clamor to get some. Everyone wants a piece of the action. It's true that you're battling a little with other traders to get in before the next guy, so to speak. But for a lot of these stocks, I've found that there is enough volume and enough trades for many small traders like me to participate.

Wow, what a trader

In the course of my trading self-education, I chatted with lots of people online about our shared interest in trading. I want to step back for a moment to something that happened to me about a year before I turned the corner. Around this time I developed a friendship with another trader in one of those message-board kind of chat rooms.

He was doing very well, and we would chat about what we saw going on. If you have not taken part in these sorts of chat rooms, you might think that traders keep to themselves, out of fear that they'll give someone else a tip and ruin things for themselves.

I've found that there is more to be gained by chatting with the right sort of people than there is a risk that you'll somehow give away your edge. After all, we're little traders and not Elon Musk, who decides to tweet one day that he wants to buy Twitter and the market moves.

Anyway, every couple of days, one of us would contact the other one. We would sometimes compare what we had our eye on in the morning, and would talk while trading.

I found that I was getting more and more frustrated as time went on: I couldn't believe the disconnect between my trading success and his. It was year two and I'd already run out of beginner's luck. I was on a steady decline with two steps forward followed by three or four big steps backwards. This was back when I was still married and I felt a lot of pressure to turn things around quickly.

I started to feel like this trader I was chatting with was acting on my ideas faster than I could. Maybe he just had more conviction while I kept hesitating. I mentioned my dismay at how much better he was doing, and he had an idea. He said I was helping him a lot, so how about we trade like a team. I could be the research and idea guy, and he could be the main trader?

It sounded like a pretty good idea. We'd set up this little company and fund it with $50,000 ($25,000 each) so we could day trade with more buying power. He said, "Just send me the $25,000 and we'll split the profit at the end of each month." Except before I actually sent him the money, I had a little bit of a funny feeling. I decided to do some digging.

I found out that the name he had given me was not real. Determined to get to the bottom of it, I was able to find his address and his real name based on a few details he had shared in passing over our time chatting. When I Googled him, I quickly learned why he had given me a fake name. He had been arrested before, and the articles about his arrest were the first thing that popped up. His name being on the national sex offender registry appeared as a close second.

I had been a couple mouse clicks away from sending him $25,000 that I most definitely could not afford to lose. Wow. That was close. I was left feeling that I couldn't trust anyone online. This is one reason I later formed my trading community. My goal has been to create a refuge from unmoderated chat rooms where so many people hang out, including predators.

"Where's my money, Ross?"

I brought this up because—fast forward to today—I regularly hear about scammers, and *some of them pose as me!*

Someone will email me: "What the hell's going on, Ross? Where's my money? I sent you the $1,000 in cryptocurrency as you told me to, so you could trade on my behalf. What's taking you so long?"

That wasn't me they were talking to. I'm sorry they were scammed, but think about it: I post my audited brokerage statements on my website. You can see me trading on YouTube most days. What's the likelihood that I'd be reaching out to people on social media and asking them to send me $1,000, so I could take a chunk out of my day and trade that?

It's like those email spam campaigns where the widow of some prince wants to send you $13 million out of the blue. It makes no logical sense. I bring this up because I came *this close* to falling for it myself, and I don't want you to get as close as I did, especially with anyone who would pretend to be me.

The Holy Grail

I had turned the corner, and at last was seeing regular green days and weeks, but I was not done with refining my approach. Because I limited myself to a short trading window in the morning, I had a lot of time during the day to think while I painted the house, chopped more wood, and whatnot.

I had come across some software that allowed for automated trading. You could script a strategy, and it would trade for you. This seemed to be really very cool.

I mean, my problem early on had been sloppy, emotion-driven trading that did not stay within strict parameters. Well, computers are all about following detailed commands. I could now tell a computer to follow all the strict parameters that I wanted, and it would never deviate from that set. It was the ultimate way to take emotion and inefficiency out of the equation and in effect have The Terminator do my trading for me.

I could program in many criteria, like:
- Percentage change on the day
- Volume relative to a stock's average volume

- The price range I want to trade in (for example, under $20 a share but not less than $2 per share)
- Total volume
- Rate of change
- Volume in the last five minutes
- Number of cents that it moved up in the last five minutes
- The spread of the stock (more on this later)

I could tell the system to scan all stocks, all the time. If it found one that met my criteria, then I could direct it to place an order for a certain amount of shares, with a fifteen-cent trailing stop. (Again, don't worry about the jargon. I'll explain it all later.)

This was amazing. And it got better: The system allowed me to take my set of trading parameters and see how well I would have done if I had that system in place during the previous thirty days of real trading activity. This was sort of an insurance policy: I might think that my parameters were good, but how well would they have done if they were in place during the last thirty days? This application of rules to historical data is known as "back testing."

> **"I tested my new system and discovered that back-testing was one thing, and actual trading was another."**

I back tested my set of rules and was like, *Wow. Over the last thirty days, if I was trading my set of rules with 1,000-share orders, I would have made twenty grand!*

This was it. Yeah, it's work to refine these criteria, but after I did the work just once, I'd be able to rely on the computer to faithfully and perfectly execute my instructions. No complaints, no sick days, and no forgetting about my explicit commands. The Holy Grail!

Too bad the real world was different. I tested my new system and discovered that back-testing was one thing, and actual trading was another. Back-tested results captured a few details about how the markets performed, but they did not record the extraordinary complexity of the minute-by-minute market. It's as if the back testing showed you a video in black and white, and when you ran those commands in the real world, you were seeing a million shades of color.

I discovered that "slippage" was the biggest variable. That is the difference between the price that you want or expect a stock to trade when you issue a command to "buy 1,000 shares *now*" and what the actual price is for that trade. The back-test results didn't factor in any slippage but in reality, on many of the trades I was taking, I was getting a lot of slippage.

The reality is the stock market is like a flowing river. You're standing there, in the river, with your fishing rod. You cast the rod intending to land your hook and bait in a certain spot, but you end up being one foot south of the spot you were looking at. That happens with the stock market, believe it or not. Humans operate in time intervals of days, hours, minutes, and seconds. The stock market operates in intervals of milliseconds (one thousandth of a second) and microseconds (one millionth of a second). What most people—including me, back then—do not realize is *stocks can trade in microseconds*. That means if another trade gets executed at 14 millionths of a second before my trade, I could pay a higher price on my order.

I discovered that there were other reasons my carefully crafted set of criteria did not work as I expected when I let it loose in the real world: it was possible that my order to buy 1,000 shares was not executed because the markets jumped over my order, and executed someone else's order that came in around the same few millionths of a second.

Alas. I had thought that I'd found the Holy Grail where I could tune and refine my criteria such that the robot system would follow my exact instructions. It did indeed follow those instructions, but the far more complex and chaotic systems that operated on millionths of seconds delivered different results.

My concept had merit, but the success of it depended on designing systems that could handle a great deal more of the behavior that happened in those millionths of seconds.

I was using impressive software, but it cost me a paltry $99 per month. In effect, I was trying to play on the same field as the Big Boys like Goldman Sachs, Morgan Stanley, and Citadel. Except they hired brilliant physicists and mathematicians and spent hundreds of millions of dollars to create their high-frequency trading systems. Those systems do indeed extract billions of dollars of profits from the stock market.

I could not play in their league. I didn't have the experience or the money to hang with them. That was the bad news, but I realized that there was also good news: I could still play the game, and win. I would just have to be content with doing it on my own, at the rate of two hours a day.

That thought gave me a type of peace. The giants could clash overhead and compete for the billions of dollars at stake in the market at large. Let them have at it. I was content to compete where the stakes were, first, my cost of living, then a nest egg, and if I played my cards right, a few million dollars in the bank. My big dreams would not even register as a blip on the screens of the Big Boys, and that was fine with me.

Thinking out loud

Earlier I mentioned that I come from a long line of teachers and teaching seems to be in my blood. I like to share what I know, and I also get clarity from putting my thoughts into words.

Throughout my early years in the market, I had gotten into the routine of answering questions beginner traders were posting in a day trading forum. I rather enjoyed the focused isolation of my solitary life in Vermont, but I also found energy in discussing day trading with others in the forum who were as passionate as I was.

During this time I decided to fence off a little corner of cyberspace that would be dedicated to day trading. I created a website, which was a fun and easy side project given my prior experience building websites. It became a bit of a digital journal where I documented the ups and downs as I was learning to trade. I also wrote articles based on common questions I would see beginner traders ask.

Like many of the websites I'd created for myself in the past, I had no business plan. I didn't quite realize it at the time, but I was building a sort of centralized database for everything related to day trading: from terminology and chart patterns, to detailed explanations of hot keys and order routing. I never found a resource with this sort of focus just on day trading when I was starting out. Even though my website was new, I began to rank well in Google for very specific keywords like "momentum day trading strategies," or "bull flag patterns." That led to people finding me and engaging with my site.

I then decided to point an inexpensive camera in my direction and hit "record" when I was trading. I embedded videos on my website and uploaded them to my new YouTube account.

It never felt like work to do the blog posts and videos, because I was just talking about the stuff I was already passionate about. This type of exposure also did not trigger anxiety attacks, because I was in my comfort zone while doing it.

Pretty soon it became clear that others were passionate about the same thing, and I developed a following. I always responded to questions and comments, and I noticed there were a ton of questions about all the tools and platforms I was using in my trading. Soon I realized I could earn affiliate revenue by providing special referral links for people who bought the same tools I was using. Even better, people who bought with my special link would typically get a discount.

I liked this model a lot, because it did not cost my viewers anything extra for me to earn the affiliate income. I was not pushing any products on anyone, and the concept was: *Here's what I use, and why I like it over the alternatives. You're free to ignore my opinion and use a different tool. But if you decide to buy it, feel free to use my link below; it'll save you X percent and I'll earn a small commission.*

I got a trickle of affiliate revenue, and then a bit more.

My goal was to make $1,000 a week in trading profits. With my small-but-growing following on social media, I thought it would be amazing if I could get to $1,000 per month in revenue from the blog. That would give me a week's worth of trading cushion every month. It was a great feeling that even if I was having a bad day trading, I didn't have to freak out because I had this little bit of affiliate revenue coming in regularly.

Upward spiral

Not only had I turned the corner, but I was picking up speed. My trading was getting more consistent and my affiliate revenue was growing.

By 2014, I had generated enough visitors to the website that I created a free chat room. Naturally, this was a chat room dedicated to day trading. As the community of active members grew, so did the demand for me to be live broadcasting during the trading day. In order to upgrade the chat room features, I discontinued the free service, and created a monthly subscription for a chat room membership.

Later that same year, I taught the first edition of my day trading course. I taught that class on repeat, once a month, for over a year.

In 2015 I wrote an earlier version of the book you are reading now. It was designed to accompany the first edition of my day trading course. It was more of a technical introduction to trading, and didn't go much into exactly what steps you should take to determine if day trading was for you, or all the things you could do to minimize your risk and build your confidence. The book you're reading now does all of that, and more.

During this period I met a great lady, and after a while we got married. She was from New York, and I was from Vermont, so we looked for a place to settle down that was roughly in between. We settled on Great Barrington, Massachusetts. Today, we have two wonderful boys, and I have the dream setup: I can take part in the crazy high-tech world of minute-by-minute day trading, while looking out my window at a backyard filled with birds, chipmunks, and the occasional fox.

Throwing down the gauntlet

Over time, my blog posts and YouTube videos led to my having something of a following in the small-cap day trading community. This following grew as I became more successful as a trader and also as I produced more courses, tools, and other information.

One of the most-common questions I got was along the lines of: "It's cool that you've become successful, but the world has changed since you made the bulk of your money. How do I know your success was not a fluke?" Other variations were more blunt: "I'd like to see if you could make any money if you were essentially starting from scratch, the way *I am*."

I thought those were reasonable questions. The world is indeed filled with so much fake stuff, what with movies containing computer-generated

> "I'd like to see if you could make any money if you were essentially starting from scratch, the way *I am*."

action adventure scenes, to outlandish claims on the internet, and so on. I think that sometimes there are people who will look for every excuse not to believe things. For example, there are still deniers about whether we actually landed astronauts on the moon despite abundant evidence of the missions. But maybe you're one of those people who is not cynical but merely skeptical or questioning, in which case, good for you! Before you invest much time and effort into something as challenging as day trading, you should get your questions answered.

"I began the account on January 1, 2017 with $583.15. In 45 days I had turned it into over $100,000. In 2019 I crossed $1,000,000 and in 2022 I crossed $10,000,000."

To answer this whole category of questions, I decided to see if I could grow an account from the minimum. As I mentioned earlier, you can't day trade in the US with an account that falls below $25,000 because you're severely restricted in how many transactions you can execute. However, several other countries have different rules and also have access to US stock markets. It's possible to open a foreign account with as little as $500 and day trade in the US.

I set a challenge for myself to trade with a tiny account. I deposited a little more than $500 in the account. After some setup fees and such, I had $583.15 available to trade.

I won't take you through the play-by-play of each of my trades during that challenge, though you can get more information from the audited brokerage statement on my website here.[3]

The big picture is that I began the account on January 1, 2017 with $583.15. In 45 days I had turned it into over $100,000. In 2019 I crossed $1,000,000 and in 2022 I crossed $10,000,000. I continue to trade in this account today.

Though I'm proud of the result, it's really important that you put this challenge in the proper perspective and understand that my results are not typical:

- The fact that I did it does not mean that "anyone can do it."
- Even though I started the account with $500, it was not the first $500 that I invested in trading, and it definitely was not my first rodeo. You will remember that I had literally spent

---

[3] https://www.warriortrading.com/583-to-1mil/

years learning how to trade. It was regularly a painful and humbling process.

- There is a certain amount of luck involved in trading. In other words, it's impossible to remove all randomness. Therefore, I could have started another challenge the next day, and it might have performed differently.

It's great if you are inspired by my challenge so that you learn more about day trading. That's why I did it.

But as we'll discuss more later, it makes no sense for you to attempt to mimic the trades I take on any given day. That's called *mirror trading*, and although many of those gurus and newsletter services will encourage you to blindly follow their alerts, I actively discourage the practice. What makes sense for anyone wanting to try to trade like me is to mimic the principles and techniques I use to trade, including the strategy, the tools, what to look for, problems to avoid, and so on. That's the whole point of this book.

Takeaways

This has been a long chapter about how I got into day trading. You might conclude that I had some advantages that you don't have, like an inheritance. I won't deny that. Then again, it would be reasonable to conclude that I had some unique disadvantages in the form of my decidedly unsupportive first wife, panic attacks, no formal training in investments, and so on.

Each of us is dealt a set of strong and weak cards. What counts is whether you decide to throw away the weak cards, get some new ones, and how you play that hand. Luck and skill will decide the outcome. What I love about day trading is how luck may always play a part, but there's nothing stopping you from working hard to increase your skills.

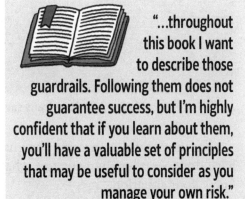

"...throughout this book I want to describe those guardrails. Following them does not guarantee success, but I'm highly confident that if you learn about them, you'll have a valuable set of principles that may be useful to consider as you manage your own risk."

In a sense, it's up to you to **un**-level the playing field in your favor through what you learn about this great business.

Guardrails

Earlier in this chapter I described how I created a set of guardrails, based on my experience and urgent need to turn my trading results around. That concept was so important to my survival and success in this business that throughout this book I want to describe those guardrails. Following them does not guarantee success, but I'm highly confident that if you learn about them, you'll have a valuable set of principles that may be useful to consider as you manage your own risk.

Figure 2-2: Guardrails save financial lives, too

I'm purposefully phrasing the guardrails as what I did—or should have done—rather than suggest what you should do, because I don't know your situation.

I'll make the first guardrail be about the five common denominators I mentioned earlier in this chapter. They are the characteristics of the stocks that I had the most success trading.

— GUARDRAIL #1 —

My stock-scanning system for momentum day trading: I focus on stocks with the following characteristics:

1. Up over 10 percent on the day versus the previous day's closing price.
2. High relative volume (at least 2.0).
3. Share prices are between $2 and $10, and not more than $20.
4. News or some other catalyst is announced today.
5. Relatively low float and therefore greater volatility (preferably twenty million shares or fewer).

We're not quite ready to roll up our sleeves and learn the technical aspects of day trading. That's because we don't have a clean slate to work from. Instead, we have a bunch of preconceptions and misconceptions about day trading that can get in the way of learning about how best to approach this business. In other words, we have a few elephants in the room.

In the next chapter, let's do some elephant hunting.

CHAPTER 3

"Day Trading is a Scam!"

DID YOU KNOW that only nine cities in America have a population of more than one million people? Well now you do.

My YouTube channel has more than a million people, which kinda makes me the mayor of a pretty large city.

As mayor, I get to deal with a certain number of lunatic citizens who make bizarre demands and will never be satisfied. They should move to another city.

But by and large, I get a lot of great questions from our community. That's part of the reason I continue to run for mayor of my YouTube channel: I get questions that keep me on my toes, and make me think in different ways.

It's possible that a few of the following questions have crossed your mind. In some cases, you may have not a question, but a belief about what day trading involves. Either way, leave your rotten tomatoes at home and let's have a town hall, where I'll give you straight responses to your toughest questions and remarks.

"If it IS possible to day trade profitably, why haven't the giant trading firms taken it over and monopolized it by this point?"

That is indeed a fair question. Here's the short answer:

Day trading is small potatoes. There just isn't enough money in it for them.

Let's take one savvy investor as an example. Here's what a financial writer said about Warren Buffett:

Buffett—and every other billionaire investor and institutional player—is essentially banned from investing in the most explosive opportunities in any meaningful way.

Let's say Buffett wanted to invest in a small-cap company valued at $1 million. He could legally invest a few thousand dollars and *hopefully, watch it soar to $100,000 or more.*

But that would be a pittance for Berkshire Hathaway, which is a juggernaut valued at hundreds of billions of dollars today. A home run on a small investment won't move the needle for Buffett.

His other option would be to invest far more—say $500,000. But then he would own so much of the company that he would need to file a 13D Schedule form with the Securities & Exchange Commission and take on the headaches that come with being what is legally known as a "beneficial owner."[4]

The giant trading firms are no different. They're looking to make the most money from the largest opportunities, and no one is stopping them. For a firm with billions of dollars of capital to invest, day trading would be stepping over dollars to pick up pennies, so to speak. Why bother with trying to make a dime or even a dollar per share, when you could invest $250 million in Tesla and possibly return a $25 million profit, or 10 percent, in a matter of months in a well-timed position?

Institutional trading firms have an undeniable edge in the market. They know—better than you or I could ever know—the inner workings of these Fortune 500 companies. They personally know executives and company owners, as they mingle at social events. They have the best analysts working to predict the future price of these companies. And the stakes are high when billions of dollars in assets are under management.

To help put this in perspective, let's look at Larry, a day trader. He opens a $25,000 account and let's say he produces $100,000 in profit in one year by trading stocks priced between $2 and $20, as they move up at least ten percent on high relative volume. Of course that performance is NOT TYPICAL, but I'm making a math point here. He's produced a 400 percent return against his $25k in starting capital. Way to go, Larry!

Let's say that Larry has a *very* rich friend, Christina, who wants to

---

[4] https://www.benzinga.com/startups/22/12/30206886/warren-buffett-its-a-huge-structural-advantage-not-to-have-a-lot-of-money

get in on the action. It's no problem for Christina to write a check and open a $25 million account, which she does.

It's exceedingly unlikely, in fact nearly impossible, that Christina will be capable of producing anything close to Larry's 400 percent return. That's because the small-cap markets rarely have the liquidity to support a trader entering or exiting a multi-million-dollar position within minutes. Larry has lots of room to grow his account, because positions of tens of thousands or even hundreds of thousands of dollars can be executed almost immediately. Christina will have to take just a sliver of her account and day trade with it, or else she's just going to have to fish in a much bigger stream than the one Larry's in.

What's great about the stock market is that, among all the different sectors, segments, and financial instruments, there is room for everyone. Day traders may be the little fish, relative to the big institutions, but we manage to co-exist.

"Day trading is gambling. Nothing more, nothing less."

Anyone can open a brokerage account, fund it with a deposit, and start mashing the buy and sell buttons. Doing just this, in the hope of getting rich, is gambling. Let there be no doubt: some people gamble in the stock market. That does not mean that the profession of day trading equals gambling.

What separates the professionals from the gamblers? The closest legitimate comparison to day trading and gambling would be when we look at a professional card counter at the blackjack table or a professional poker player. Both are highly trained and highly disciplined people. They know with a fair degree of statistical confidence when to hold 'em and when to fold 'em. With strategy and discipline, they can actually push the odds for long-term success in their favor.

Day trading is very similar in this way. Those who approach trading with strategy and discipline have the best chance of pushing the odds in their favor.

"I do think there is a certain amount of beginner's luck out there. I attribute this to the confidence that can come with being incompetent."

The beauty of day trading is that there are several steps you can take to affirmatively reduce your risk. And by first reducing your risk, you can begin the process of developing strategy and discipline in a safe environment. We will cover this extensively in Chapter 8.

"What role does luck or chance have in day trading?"

You read in Chapter 2 about my friend, Ben, who made a cool $16,000 while in high school. That sort of trading is luck. And in his case, it was beginner's luck. That winner was not the culmination of strategy and discipline. He heard something, placed a trade, and it paid off. But it was a fluke, as represented by the fact that he's not still trading today.

I do think there is a certain amount of beginner's luck out there. I attribute this to the confidence that can come with being incompetent. It's the blissful ignorance of risk that leads some beginners to inadvertently take high-risk positions. If they pay off, it's beginner's luck. I was profitable in my first year of trading, probably thanks in part to some higher-risk winners, and then I gave it all back in my second year.

But luck works both ways.

As an example of bad luck, I was once trading at my farmhouse in Vermont, and a tree knocked down a utility pole. My internet and power went down, and there was no cell signal there. I had taken a position before the power went out and I was stuck! My laptop was still on, but I was offline. Frozen screen, no quotes. Panic. This could be *very* bad, depending on what the market did next.

I jumped in my car and raced down the road to an area where I thought I might be able to reach my broker on my cell phone, which I did. Fortunately, the stock had not moved a lot. That's a combination of bad and good luck, I suppose.

From that experience I learned a lesson: always have my broker on speed-dial and have multiple sources of internet or communication. Today I have both my primary internet and my computer on an uninterruptible power supply, and my cell phone serves as a hotspot for backup.

Over the long haul, luck plays less and less of a role in day trading. The real practitioners tend to stay in the business, and those who rely on good luck or hot tips tend to get washed out.

"**If it's possible for regular people to make money—consistent money—by day trading, then why isn't everyone doing it?**"

That's an easy one to answer!

Most people are **not cut out** to be day traders.

Many people who try to day trade come into the profession with severely inaccurate impressions about what it takes to day trade successfully. Some believe having a fancy financial background or exceptional intellect will make them more likely to succeed. Others think it's just a matter of hanging out on social media and jumping in on the next "meme" stock.

Even if everyone had an accurate impression of day trading, most people will not be willing to put in the time to get good at trading. And those who *are* willing to put in the time may not have the aptitude to be a successful trader.

This is an appropriate time to go over a whole bunch of "qualifications" for day trading that are over-rated or irrelevant. Then we'll talk about the real qualifications to be a trader.

IRRELEVANT BELIEF #1: *I've been told more than once that I'm "good at everything I set my mind to."* It's true that successful day trading requires a certain level of self-confidence. You can't be second-guessing yourself while your finger hovers endlessly over the "Buy" or "Sell" button. But natural talent is overrated. What's much more important is the willingness to put in the work, and to stick with it through the inevitable—yes, inevitable—down periods. Sometimes it's the "naturals" who bail out the soonest, and the scrappy, tenacious bulldogs end up being the successful ones.

IRRELEVANT BELIEF #2: *I'm great at math.* That can be helpful, but it's hardly a guarantee. No matter how great you think you are at math, computers can calculate faster than you can. Traders can set up basically any kinds of ratios and trend lines they wish, and have them calculated instantaneously in real time by the computer, so any natural mathematical gift is less and less of a competitive edge.

IRRELEVANT BELIEF #3: *Day trading should not be that tough; I have an MBA and am kick-butt at reading financial statements.* Congratulations on your hard work to get that MBA. I have some bad news for you: most of what you learned is irrelevant to becoming a good day trader. In fact, it could even lead you down the wrong path. Here's what I've come to understand:

Day trading is not about becoming expert at the stocks you will buy and sell. Day trading is about becoming an expert at human nature.

You need to become an observer of investing emotions—both yours and those of the other traders. Learning how the human emotions of fear and greed translate into price action is critical to your ability to profitably trade the markets. You need to capitalize on emotions in the market without falling victim to your own emotions. When you're looking at how a stock is behaving on an intraday basis, it's not the company that is the engine for gains and losses. Sure, the company may have issued a press release about their quarterly earnings, a new revolutionary project, or a bankruptcy.

Those are all important headlines, but contrary to popular belief, it's not the news stories that change the price of the stock. Changes in stock price are because of changes in supply and demand. Thus, changes in stock price are driven by active traders and high-frequency trading algorithms. A bankruptcy does not cause stocks automatically to change hands. What the news does is affect the emotions of traders, who then act on their fear, greed, suspicions, intuition, pride, and other strong emotions.

Check this out: Researchers studied stock-market movements after big events. In one study, they looked at the market movements after announcements of the illness or death of US presidents. Following the news, the stock market instantly reacted negatively, but then tended to bounce back the very next day. Think about that: on the bounce-back day, the president was still sick or dead, so nothing had fundamentally changed. Instead, human sentiment had collectively shifted from pessimism to optimism.[5]

Let's look at it another way: Assume for a moment that you study the financial statements of a company and also go to great lengths to examine the senior leadership of that company. You don't stop there, but then talk to industry experts and analysts about that company's products and services, and whether they're well positioned to grow.

---

[5] https://www.diva-portal.org/smash/get/diva2:727314/FULLTEXT01.pdf

Even with all of that knowledge, a small-cap stock has the potential to trade up 500 percent or 1,000 percent in the space of one day. Depending on how much you bought and sold on that day—and *exactly* when you did so—you may have done splendidly or you may have lost your butt. Same company, same senior staff, same products. As stocks squeeze up, they are experiencing massive amounts of momentum, fueled by FOMO, greed, and speculation. These emotions fuel volatility. Exaggerated moves are often reversed as emotions swing from greed during the rise to fear during the decline.

To be successful at day trading, what you need much more than a Master of Business Administration degree is a Master of Human Behavior degree.

We talked about three irrelevant things that people may think are qualifications, but that will be of little help in day trading. Here is why day trading is not for most people:

You need to pay the hard and soft costs of admission. When I say "hard cost" I mean that you'll need to fund your account with a certain amount of money. We'll talk about your account funding options in more detail later in this book. Other hard costs include the purchase of your computer and any external monitors, and the cost of any courses, chat rooms, news services, and software tools you may use.

The "soft costs" are far more expensive: These involve the significant time you will invest in learning how to day trade. Sure, nothing is stopping you from day trading on the first hour that your brokerage account is open, and with no prior training. That is a recipe for disaster in this business. Depending on how reckless you are, it could cost you far more than the money you funded your account with.

Let's assume you're willing to learn. It's not like school, where you might pull an all-nighter and pass the test. Here's what you need to do, in order to be successful in *this* real-life school:

1. You've got to first learn a lot of concepts. That takes work but is straightforward.
2. Then you need to understand how to manage your risk. This involves a set of principles that you'll apply in different situations. We'll talk about them later.

3. Next—if you're smart—you will not risk a dime, but will see how good you are in a simulator before trading in a real money account. (We'll talk much more about this tool later.) Maybe you'll be amazing at first, or awful: the market will quickly let you know.

4. It'll then be time to figure out what you're doing wrong, fix it, and try more simulator action.

5. Only when you're consistently doing at least OK should you even think about using real money. No matter how good you were in the simulator, you'll discover that trading with real money is different, so there'll be an adjustment phase.

And these steps are *only the beginning*. You'll have a long period of learning, successes, setbacks, and adjustments before you'll feel like you maybe got this thing called trading.

Now, considering all the steps I just talked about, what amount of humanity do you think will stick with it until they're competent at trading? Yeah, about a teaspoonful. The physical barriers to entry are low. The mental barriers are formidable.

I'm not trying to scare you off or paint a dark picture of the business I love. I am trying to be realistic, so you have an authentic picture at the outset.

If you want to learn a great deal about yourself and how you think and behave under pressure, study day trading. If you want a graduate degree in human nature—both yours and the traders you'll trade with—study day trading.

"If you want to learn a great deal about yourself and how you think and behave under pressure, study day trading. If you want a graduate degree in human nature—both yours and the traders you'll trade with—study day trading."

It's the craziest thing: to the rest of the world it looks like we're engaged in fancy-sounding activities relating to "high finance" or "financial markets" or "prospects for pharmaceutical advances." Instead, for the most part we're anticipating what a bunch of other humans will be thinking, feeling, and acting on in the next *five to ten minutes*.

If you're willing to pay this significant price in terms of time, money, frustration, and being humbled, you've come to the right place.

"No offense, Ross, but I have a hard time believing that you will tell me *exactly* the methods you use to trade. If you did that, wouldn't you lose your competitive edge?"

It may be hard to believe if you're not in the business, but as soon as you start to learn day trading, you'll understand why I can share everything without fear of being out-competed.

The stock market is this amazing kaleidoscope of activity. Trades are happening—even within one stock—in literally microseconds of each other. National news, local news, and company news is continuously washing over all of us investors: on any given day, are there recession fears? What battles are going on in Congress? Is the Food and Drug Administration authorizing some new drug? Did war break out somewhere? The list is endless.

The "secrets" I try to emphasize relate to things like:

- How to manage your emotions when you're doing great and think you're invincible; or when you've had a string of red days, think you know nothing, and are ready to throw in the towel.
- How to get continuously better at recognizing patterns you've seen before, at seeing new patterns, and at ignoring extraneous stuff.
- A whole lot of ways to manage the risk you're taking.
- How to know when to keep trading and when to shut it down.

These are just a handful of my "secrets." I'm completely willing to discuss them at length, because so few people will take the time and effort to internalize them. Even if they do, there's more than enough profit in the markets to go around.

Some people have a scarcity mindset, also known as "zero sum": they think that if they make a profitable trade, someone else loses. I disagree. First, if I make money on a trade, I have no idea how long the person on the other side of that trade held the stock for, and what price they got in at.

Second, the markets are a vast ocean of money, measured in many trillions of dollars. If you dip your kiddie spoon in the ocean, or a big bucket, or a swimming pool, it doesn't change the water level for the rest of us.

"Ross, I know you did a challenge in 2017 where you turned $583 into more than ten million dollars.[6] Bet you can't do that again! After all, the world has turned upside down since then."

For me, the hardest part of any small account challenge is making the first $25,000. Beyond that, I feel like it's not a matter of whether I can turn it into millions of dollars—it's just a matter of when I cross that line.

Why is that first $25,000 the hardest part? In a small trading account I have zero cushion. If I start with $500, and simply have the misfortune of starting with an eight- or ten-trade losing streak, there is a good chance I'll have to add more money to the account. Does that mean I've failed the challenge? Perhaps. But trading isn't a sprint, it's a marathon. I always get back on the horse and try again.

The reason I don't reset my trading account to $500 at the beginning of each month is because of the tremendous opportunity cost of trading with such a small account. It's simply not possible to make as much with a $500 account as I can with a $50,000 or $500,000 account.

For me, trading with a $500 account is really about proof of concept. Does the strategy work? Can I produce profit? It's not about doing the same thing over and over.

Think back to when you learned how to drive. You first studied the book about driving rules, and watched other people as they navigated different situations. All of that was vital to your preparation. But after a certain point, your next big learning moment came when you got behind the wheel. There is nothing quite like learning by trial and error. With learning to drive, trial and error is hopefully within the safe environment of a driving instructor sitting next to you. And let's hope it's not in an expensive car.

The trading simulator is like the driving instructor, making sure

---

[6] Just because these were my results, it doesn't mean you will do the same. My results are not typical. Don't be in a rush! You can see my audited performance here: https://www.warriortrading.com/ross-camerons-verified-day-trading-earnings/

you don't get wrecked. Trading in a $500 account is like driving your first car. You'll make beginner mistakes, but the damage is minimal in a small account. Spend all the time you need in that safe environment where the stakes are low. Once you've proven consistency, confidence will follow. That's when it's time to scale up to a larger account.

"I'm intrigued by the whole concept of day trading. You're good at this stuff. Just so you know a little about me, I've been a computer nerd for a long time. I'm *incredibly fast* with the keyboard. Why can't I skip all the concepts and learning, and simply follow you as you trade?"

What you're proposing is known as "mirror trading." My strong recommendation is that you do not bother to try it, for several reasons:

First, I've been at this profession for a while and my risk tolerance may not be the same as yours. I'll make judgments about what I should do that may differ significantly from what would be prudent for you to do. In some situations, I might decide on the spot that I can take the risk of losing $50,000, which could be no big deal for me but it could wipe you out.

Second, what you don't realize is you **cannot trade fast enough to be exactly like me.** It's not that I'm some keyboard wizard that can hit the keys faster than anyone else on the planet. It's because the financial markets these days are measured literally in **millionths of a second**—microseconds—while a simple blink of your eye takes many thousands of times longer. Even *if I wanted to*, I could not follow some other trader in real time and hope to get the exact same prices. We humans are competing against machines that can execute orders a thousand times faster than we can.

Third, *what do you learn* by mimicking me? If you are suited to this profession—and only a small percentage of people are suited— you must become self-sufficient at finding and executing your trades. That's what creates true independence. That's when you'll have learned how to fish on your own. It's so much better in the long run than just being fed trade alerts or blindly following somebody else.

"I really like the idea of day trading, but the reality is that I currently have a job that prevents me from trading in the morning, when the market opens. Is there still a way for me to trade successfully?"

That's a very tough question. To be honest, I cannot think of a day trader who trades only in the afternoon and who has done well in this business. Maybe they exist, but I'm drawing a blank. In terms of volume, the vast majority of trades occur in the first few hours of trading, from 7:30 am to 11:30 am Eastern Time. Trading happens at other hours, but that morning window is when most of the action happens.

I know traders who have side hustles, and who can trade in the morning and then do their other business for the rest of the day. If you simply cannot be available to trade in the morning, you're going to have a really tough time. I'm not saying that it's impossible to become profitable, but it will be very much more difficult than if you're available in the morning. This is also not to say that you couldn't practice in the evenings or on the weekends on replay data, but when it's time to test the waters with real money, you'll need to be available for the morning trading sessions.

"Can day trading ever be made safe?"

No. I can't predict the future of artificial intelligence and other technologies, but from where I sit, day trading is always going to involve risk. At a fundamental level, you are trying to predict what a bunch of strangers and algorithms are going to do in the next few minutes. You can apply a great deal of experience and risk-mitigation techniques to lessen that risk, but it will never entirely go away.

"I like what I've heard about day trading, but I really am skeptical about my chances. I'm not some Red Bull swilling alpha male, but I'm a woman. On top of that…"

Whoa, hold your horses! This is shaping up to be a great question, and I want to answer it more completely in the next chapter. Hold that thought!

CHAPTER 4

The Market Does Not Care

OKAY, WE'RE BACK. At the end of the last chapter, you were asking me a great question. Here is the question in full, and my answer in full:

"I like what I've heard about day trading, but I really am skeptical about my chances. I'm not some Red Bull swilling alpha male, but I'm a woman. On top of that, I've never thought of myself as being good at math. And by the way, English is my second language. Tell it to me straight: Am I screwed?"

No, you are not. The amazing thing about the day trading business is that it's agnostic: It does not care about your race, ethnicity, age, or political persuasion. It only cares about your actions: when you buy or sell, and for how much. You will be judged on your performance. Period.

It's a simple fact that most day traders are guys. Fortunately, you can trade from your computer as much as you wish and never set foot in some boiler room of the sort that was featured in the movie *The Wolf of Wall Street*. In fact, people don't have to know what gender, race, and age you are, unless you tell them.

Look, there are people in this business who shouldn't be. Lots of them. They see some tweet from a guy claiming to have made a ton of money on the "next GameStop" and how you're "gonna regret it if you don't get in now!!!!" Next thing you know they are caught up in thinking about how much they could make and they carelessly invest their life savings. This is what I would define as gambling, and unfortunately it's more common than you might think.

I'll be happy if my book persuades some of these impressionable people to not get in the business, because I've opened their eyes to how hard real day trading is.

One of the main reasons I wrote this book is to connect with people who think day trading *cannot* work for them, but they are wrong. They're curious, or else they would not bother to pick up a book about day trading in the first place. However, they're five percent curious and about 95 percent sure that day trading can't work for them. In this short chapter

I want to talk to you, if what I said sounds like you.

First, I want to acknowledge that there is no "level playing field" for all investors at all times. It's true that giant banks and trading firms have big advantages over us little folks. They have vast amounts of money to spend, and they hire armies of PhDs in mathematics, physics, and computer science. Then they spend a bundle on their data centers so they can trade—not as fast as "humanly possible"—but as fast as the fastest computers can possibly trade.

So let's stipulate all that. Even so, day trading is an amazingly fair platform for the rest of us. Consider the following:

- **There is no entrance exam to start trading.** Contrast that with so many professions where membership fees and exams are ways to control how many people can be "certified." Of course, people should still take day trading seriously and study it! There is a great deal to learn, even if there are no formal certifications for it.

- **The stock market does not care about the color of your skin,** your gender, or ethnicity.

- **It does not care whether you graduated from Harvard** or never went to high school.

- **The market does not care how famous or rich your parents are.** If you're going to succeed as a trader, it will be on your own.

- **The market does not care whether you're using a \$10,000 water-cooled computer versus a used laptop,** though it's true that having a couple of cheapo extra monitors will make your life easier, and a computer that crashes in the middle of a trade would create unnecessary risk. In Chapter 5, I'll describe the minimum setup you need to trade efficiently, but it's not expensive gear.

- **There is no casino-style "house"** that will give you free drinks and show tickets if you blow a lot of money, or that will throw you out of the casino if you use every tool at your disposal to buy and sell shares—and you win.

This concept of a non-caring market also has its sobering aspects:

- **The market does not care if you *deserve* to do well,** because you've always been a kind person who's led a virtuous life of helping others. You place your trades and you will experience the consequences.

- **The market is not the least-bit impressed that you absolutely kicked ass yesterday** and made more in your trades than most people make in a year. Nor does it care if you screwed up big-time yesterday. Today's a new day and yesterday no longer counts.

- **The market does not care how hard you are trying, or how long you've been studying.** Your buy and sell orders either produce profit, or they don't.

- **You cannot reason with the market,** or appeal a decision because, for example, you acted on market news that turned out to be a fake press release that pretended to be some Food and Drug Administration announcement of a cancer cure. You decided to buy and sell, and your decision was final.

These positive and negative consequences of a non-caring market may put off many people. However, I've found that things attract to the extent that they also repel. For people who've been put down or disadvantaged in some way in their lives, the day trading market provides a place where you can be judged purely on your actions, if you're willing to work hard and learn the craft. For some people, that place can be a relief and even a sanctuary.

When I applied (unsuccessfully) to be an intern at a hedge fund in New York City, I was not on a level playing field. I had no family connections, no prestigious college degree, and no prior hedge fund experience. But when I chose the path of day trading, I was able to prove success on my own merits.

CHAPTER 5

The Gear You'll Need

IN CHAPTER 3 I REFERRED TO SOME "HARD COSTS" OF ADMISSION to the day trading community. Before we get into much more detail about concepts and principles of day trading, we should make sure that you can cover these costs.

You'll need a computer. Many people are surprised that I do all of my trading on a laptop. They think I must have some water-cooled beast of a custom-gaming desktop rig. I guess if it makes you feel badass, then go ahead and get that gear. I like the feeling of being able to travel with the same laptop I use at home. I got my first laptop in 1999, and I haven't looked back. Laptops for life.

You don't need one of the highest-end laptops, but it needs a decent graphics card so you can run two or three external monitors. I like Lenovo Legion and Falcon laptops, but I'm sure other manufacturers make plenty-powerful ones.

It's easiest if you run Windows.[7] All the older legacy trading software was designed for Windows. A lot of brokers still only offer Windows software. However, that's changing. If you open accounts at certain bigger brokers like E*TRADE or Ameritrade, you can use MacOS just as well. The smaller brokers are still playing catch up with rolling out software for MacOS.

You'll do well to have a couple of external monitors. Confession time: at one point, I had ten monitors running simultaneously, powered by three computers. I thought that might allow me to *really see* what was going on in the markets. Over time, I found that to be not the case, because I reached the point of cognitive overload. I need to have an uncluttered brain when I'm making trading decisions. Therefore, my minimum arrangement is I have two external monitors when

---

[7] In case you're not sure what I'm talking about, the world is divided into basically two camps: those that run computers that are based in the Microsoft Windows world, and those that run Apple Macintosh and other Apple systems that use what's known as "MacOS." Yes there's also Linux, but I don't know any trading systems that use it.

I'm traveling. I currently like ASUS USB monitors for my traveling trading station. They are not fancy "4K" resolution, but simply 1080p. They hook up to my laptop via USB connectors, and I have clips to attach the monitors to the side of my laptop screen.

On the left monitor I have my scanners that show me which stocks are really active at the moment, and I have a chart of the one stock that I'm trading. On my center laptop monitor, I have my brokerage window up, along with the Warrior Trading chat room window. On the right monitor, I have two more stocks that I'm watching. That gives me a total of two stocks I can watch and one stock I'm trading. These three stocks will typically be the top three leading percentage gainers in the market on that day.

When I'm home, I don't use the USB monitors that clip onto my laptop, but I have 24" ASUS HDMI monitors that sit on a multi-monitor stand. I also have a fourth monitor that has two more stocks that I'm watching. (In other words, three monitors and my laptop.) So at home I have four stocks that I'm watching, and one that I'm trading. I've found this to be the sweet spot of plenty of information without overload.

You will need to open a brokerage account. This will be where you execute trades. I don't want to name companies in this book, because the list changes from time to time. If you want to know which firms I think are acceptable, I suggest you go to this page[8] and you will see more information there.

You should use a simulator. Certain brokers offer simulators to their clients. I like the simulator that you can access from here.[9] You may find other simulators that you like, but it is vital that you use one! It's reckless to be a beginner at day trading and not build your skills using a simulator.

Whichever one you go with, it should have at least four characteristics:

1. **Real-time data.** You want the simulator to protect you from losing real money, but it must not be *similar* to the stock market—it needs to reflect the *actual* stock market.

2. **Level 2 data.** Level 2 data allows you to see the depth of the market. This is important when you're learning to trade. We'll discuss this in more detail later on.

3. **Hot keys.** Though I sometimes trade with a mouse, I can trade much faster with hot keys. They can be programmed to do various functions with the click of a button.

4. **Trading history.** It's crucial that you are able to export your trading history to analyze your previous trades. As we'll discuss in Chapter 11, this is one of the best ways for you to improve over time.

── GUARDRAIL #2 ──

I should have used a simulator and proven that I could be profitable there before ever risking a dime of real money.

I made that mistake at first, but you don't have to. I also get the occasional objection along the lines of: "I don't use simulators because it's too easy to trade with fake money. I want to really learn the business by having real money on the line." I still think that's reckless for almost all people. If you have a trust fund or a business that's doing well, maybe you're fine with losing $20k or $30k. For the rest of us, the

---

[8] https://www.warriortrading.com/bookbonus/

[9] https://www.warriortrading.com/paper-trading/

shortest and least-painful way to learn the profession is to get good at simulated trading. Then you can transition to real-money trading. Not only will the simulator save you from losses while you're learning the basics, but it will boost your confidence once you can produce green days consistently.

An even worse objection is when somebody says "Ross, I can't afford to spend time trading in a simulator, I need to make money right away." Let me be the first to tell you that this mindset is setting you up for failure. Traders who come into the market needing to make money quickly will typically speed through the process, put undue pressure on themselves, and begin a rapid downward spiral. If you need money quickly, there are a million better ways to do it. With trading, you have to focus on the process, not the profits.

> "If you need money quickly, there are a million better ways to do it. With trading, you have to focus on the process, not the profits."

You need software to show you what to focus on. I'm a momentum trader, meaning that I am not interested in what stock *might* be poised to move up, or *might* be undervalued. I focus on the stocks that are moving *right now*. By using stock scanners, I'm working smarter, not harder. I don't need to research every undervalued company, read hundreds of pages of financial statements, or evaluate the opinions of various analysts.

You need software that shows you which stocks are making the biggest moves, which ones have the most trading volume, the highest relative volume, a valid news catalyst, and of course the right float. I have my custom scanners that I make available to my community, but you could get software from other providers. No matter from whom you get them, you must have scanners.

Get a reliable internet connection and a second way to connect. We've all suffered from bad internet connections. I can tell you from personal experience that the fastest way to shoot your blood pressure through the roof is to have a connection that goes down in the middle of a trade. In Chapter 3, I described just this sort of internet outage.

If you are "short" a position, you can lose a great deal of mon-

ey—career-ending money—if you
cannot act quickly enough to "cover" your position. Regard it as cheap
insurance to spend a few dollars
per month on a separate internet
hookup that you can switch to at a
moment's notice. If you want to get
fancy, you can even connect multiple internet service providers into a
load balancing router so you have
a failsafe without having any loss
of connectivity.

> **"I don't care how fast of a learner you are. You will not live long enough, or have enough money, to make all the mistakes yourself that you can make in this business."**

You need a support system. Otto Von Bismarck, the German statesman, said: "Fools say 'experience is the best teacher.' I prefer to learn from other people's experience." I don't care how fast of a learner you are. You will not live long enough, or have enough money, to make all the mistakes yourself that you can make in this business.

Even if you are lucky enough to be brilliant, *and* hard-working, *and* patient, you will find that day trading is hard. The only things that carry over from yesterday and your trading past are the knowledge and skills you decide to apply. A trading community helps you to apply what you know and stay disciplined.

Warrior Trading has a great community and excellent resources, but no one has a monopoly on such things. If you find some other group that seems to offer the tools, knowledge, information, and sup-port that fits best with your personality and needs—go for it. Just be sure to find *something* that meets a set of minimum criteria.

What are those criteria?

The first function of that system is to be a place where you can get **well-informed answers to your specific technical questions about day trading.** X or Reddit don't qualify. It's too easy for people to dip in and out, brag, talk trash, and vanish. Find a group that's led by people who can prove that they're successful at day trading, and not people who simply brag with no proof.

Second, find a place where their **software tools and strategies align with your risk tolerance, personality, and current knowledge.** If you're learning momentum day trading that's focused on small-cap stocks, the tools and community should be largely following the same trading profile as yours.

Third, look for a group where you find a compatible chemistry so that you derive support and inspiration from them. In case you hadn't gathered something about me by now, I'm not a big extrovert. Even so, I believe it's critical to take part in an online community of like-minded people.

It's been said that you become like the people you surround yourself with. There are communities with personalities that thrive on bullying, negativity, and hostility. These communities are not conducive to learning. It's not hard to tell ones that have a foundation in positivity versus negativity.

Ultimately you are alone when you hit the "Enter" key to buy and sell shares. You sink or swim on the instant judgments you make. But you can reduce your risk of making irrational decisions by listening to the regular thoughts and perspectives of other traders whose opinions you've come to respect.

Of course, this process takes time. At first you won't be sure about who thinks and acts similarly to the way you do. But if you get in the right group, you'll come to value the support and sense of shared mission.

——■——

This chapter has been about the minimum gear you'll need in order to begin your trading journey. The next chapter will cover some knowledge you must have before you even think about placing your first trade.

CHAPTER 6

Stock Market Basics

OF COURSE I CANNOT TEACH YOU EVERYTHING I know about day trading and somehow cram it into one volume. But what I can do in this book is teach you everything *you need to know*, in order to be well-informed about the day trading road you're considering.

In the last chapters I've already thrown around several terms like "small cap" and "swing trading." Perhaps you already know how the stock market works, in which case you can skip this chapter. If that is not the case, then buckle up, because we're about to cover a whole lot of material in a hurry.

You and I start a business

Let's say for this chapter that I'm back in Vermont. You and I knew each other from high school and we reconnected at a reunion. Turns out we've both enjoyed Ben & Jerry's ice cream for years, and both of us had sent in ideas for flavors but those ideas fell on deaf ears. After a while we decided to open a small ice cream shop, then another, and now we have eight more! People adore our flavors. We've got a tiger by the tail here.

We definitely want to grow this thing as large as we can make it, but merely reinvesting our profits is inhibiting our plans. It's nice and safe but we see an opportunity that won't last forever, so we need to grow much faster than we can fund ourselves.

Equity versus debt

We have some options. We could do debt financing, in the form of a bank loan. That's okay, but we realized that the interest payments would kill our profit margin. Furthermore, the debt repayment comes right off the top of our revenues, meaning that we must repay the bank before paying any of our other expenses.

We decide we need to preserve our profit margin, but are willing to share the wealth in another way. We want to do an equity offering. The bad news with giving someone else equity is we're sharing in the ownership of the company. At least with debt, the bank gets its slice of money and no more. If we do well, we don't have to share those extra profits with the bank. But if we're having a hard time, the bank does not care: it wants its money. They required us to put up the land under our shops as collateral, so if we don't pay, they can grab the land, sell it, and there goes our business.

By sharing equity, we in effect are taking on money partners who will share in all the profits we make. On the other hand, if we have a big expansion year and there are few profits, they will take nothing off the top, but will get smaller checks, just like us founders.

A brief note about debt offerings. If we're a big company, we could decide to issue bonds, which is another form of debt. There is a whole spectrum of types of bonds. Large companies—and even the US government—issue bonds. Some are senior to other types of debt, meaning that they must be repaid before the others. There are even bonds known as debentures, which are not backed by any collateral. They will be repaid only if the company has the funds. Why would anyone buy such bonds? Because they come with a great interest rate. The more risk investors are willing to take about getting repaid, the higher the interest rate they can expect.

Types of equity

Now that we decided to do an equity offering, we have a choice: private or public. If you follow the financial news, you hear about "private equity firms" all the time. They can write a big check quickly and then suddenly have a big say in how the company operates. It's similar to venture capital (or the "Shark Tank" show), where you maybe get $1.5 million in a funding round, in exchange for 10 percent ownership in the company. In that scenario, your company is valued at $15 million because a 10 percent slice cost $1.5 million.

Private equity is called "private" because there are no shares available on stock exchanges. It was a private transaction. Instead, we decide to go public. That means we want to sell shares in our company and have them listed on an exchange. The first time a company issues public stock is known as an IPO, or Initial Public Offering. The world's most famous stock exchange is the New York Stock Exchange, or NYSE. At first, it was pretty much the only game in town, but that's changed, along with the rest of modern life. Now there are 13 stock exchanges in the US alone.[10] The 16 largest stock exchanges in the world each have a capitalization of more than $1 trillion.[11]

A word about public companies: when you go public, you'll be forever scrutinized by stock analysts. Some of them are incredibly experienced and knowledgeable professionals who are true experts in certain industries. Others are fresh out of business school, and the last business they ran was a lemonade stand. Either way, they'll issue analyses and earnings estimates about stocks every quarter. The true experts—and the others—issue public opinions about the company and its prospects for growth. Often a battle ensues between the analysts and the company about those future prospects. It's enough to cause some companies to avoid going public altogether, or to actually reverse a public offering and go private through a share buyback or a buyout. That's exactly what companies like Twitter (now "X") and Dell did.[12]

Types of stock

Each exchange has its own rules about the types of companies that can issue stock. Let's say we decided to list our stock on the NASDAQ, which is one of the largest exchanges in the US. We then had another decision to make—the type of stock to issue. The standard kind is known as common stock. There are other types, like preferred stock which can claim more rights in terms of the dividends and other assets of the company. There is also non-voting stock, and many other types.

Dividends

There used to be something called "widow and orphan stocks" because they paid generous dividends, which are partial payouts of the annual profits of a company. Those were also known as blue-chip stocks. The idea was that widows and orphans could survive on the income from the dividends that these stocks paid.

Some stocks pay relatively significant dividends and others pay none. Why wouldn't everyone want a stock that pays a bunch of dividends? Because that money is going out the door. Many companies

---

[10] https://app.fintrakk.com/article/how-many-stock-exchanges-usa

[11] https://en.wikipedia.org/wiki/List_of_stock_exchanges

[12] https://www.investopedia.com/articles/active-trading/073015/10-most-famous-public-companies-went-private.asp

realize they could expand and invest in better equipment and a larger staff with those dollars, instead of writing checks to stockholders. That money may make the stockholders briefly happy but it does nothing to help the business.

We decided to issue common stock and plan on paying no dividends. We want to build this company into a powerhouse ASAP, and the shareholders will thank us later as the value of the company—and the price of their shares—increases.

Details

Because you and I are experts in ice cream and not in finance, we hired an underwriter. That company knows all about stock offerings, and also when it is the best time to go public. If the US economy is currently weak, then our underwriter may advise us to hold off. After all, we want to issue stock at the highest price per share we can get. That price is partly driven by the assets we've built up in the company, and partly by the investing climate on the day we issue the shares. Pity the company that decides to offer shares when something like COVID splashes into the news: no matter how good the underlying company might be, investors will be skittish and won't want to pay much for anything.

We huddled with our underwriter and chose a date for our IPO. Part of the concept of "underwriting" is the due diligence that the underwriter performs. That's an analysis of our company and its management, prospects, and risks, among other things. The underwriter also helps with submitting a whole lot of documents to the Securities and Exchange Commission, or SEC. They have detailed requirements about the many disclosures companies must make when issuing stock.

The main document relating to our stock offering is called the prospectus. It contains an overview of the company, its management, nature of operations, known risk factors, and prior financial history. The prospectus is submitted to the SEC, which does not "approve" such filings, but acknowledges receipt of them.

Among other things, the SEC requires that we issue an annual report, also known as a 10K filing. It becomes public information when we file it and is available at the SEC's site. Quarterly reports are called 10Q filings. If we have important news to report about our company between quarterly reports, we must issue an 8K. There are many other types of filings relating to ownership, voting, and so on.

The big day

When the day actually arrives for the stock to go public, an official price per share will be set. Then the actual sale will begin for those shares.

When Apple Computer stock was being listed for the first time, there was worldwide interest in buying those shares. They were offered at $22 per share on December 12, 1980. All available shares were snapped up in minutes as trading commenced under the stock symbol AAPL. People who bought them at $22 might have thought that a quick profit of $5 per share was great, and sold their shares at $27 or whatever. Perhaps a few investors might still own Apple shares they bought at $22 per share over 40 years ago. Other shares may have traded hands several times even on that first day. By the end of the first day, they were trading at $29 per share, or almost 32 percent higher.[13]

It's important to understand what happened in this example of Apple. The company was paid $22 for each share that investors bought. That's all the money the company got from the IPO. (Though it also got a great deal of publicity, which doesn't hurt a company that sells retail products.)

Those original buyers of AAPL were able to sell the stock to other investors, who may have done the same thing to yet other investors. The result was that the marketplace had valued AAPL stock at the end of that day at $29.

Those original shares kept being valued more and more by the investing community. In fact, Apple has had a series of stock splits, where they would issue more than one share for each share you owned, albeit at lower share prices. For example, seven years later, Apple offered a 2-for-1 stock split, so each share was worth half as much, but you got two shares for each one you owned. Companies do that so their shares do not get insanely expensive on a per-share basis. Warren Buffett does not believe in stock splits, so one share of Berkshire Hathaway now costs more than $400,000.[14]

If you had bought $10,000 of Apple at the IPO and held onto those shares, it would be worth more than $14 million now.[15]

---

[13] https://www.edn.com/apple-ipo-makes-instant-millionaires-december-12-1980/

[14] https://en.wikipedia.org/wiki/Berkshire_Hathaway

[15] https://www.nasdaq.com/articles/if-you-invested-%2410000-in-apple-for-its-ipo-in-1980-heres-how-much-youd-have-now

Market capitalization

You've heard me talk about small-cap stocks. If you take the current price of a company's stock, multiplied by the number of shares the company has issued, you get market capitalization. If that number is more than $10 billion, it's called a large-cap stock. If it's from $2 billion to $10 billion, then it's called a mid-cap. And if it's between $300 million and less than $2 billion, it's a small-cap stock. The small fry below $300 million are known as micro-cap stocks, and the tiny companies under $50 million are nano-caps.

Although it's possible to day trade any stock from large-cap on down to nano-cap, as you learned in Chapter 2, I prefer to trade stocks with a limited number of shares available. This reduces the supply in the supply/demand equation.

That means I focus more on float than on market capitalization. Remember that float is the number of shares available to trade, and it comprises the shares a company issued through IPOs and secondary offerings.

When you focus on float, you'll generally find yourself trading stocks with market capitalizations of less than $1 billion. If I focus on trading stocks under $20 per share, and with a float of less than 50 million shares[16], that means the largest market cap I would typically trade is $20 x 50 million = $1 billion.

There are certainly exceptions to this. I will eagerly trade large companies including Facebook, Alibaba, Uber, Airbnb, and Snapchat on the day of their initial public offering. I might also trade them on days when they are having a once-in-a-decade type of news event that has sparked massive volatility. But generally speaking, I find more consistent volatility in stocks with smaller market caps.

Back to our stock

Let's say we completed our IPO at $10 and all our shares were purchased. That doesn't always happen, but we had a good company and good underwriter.

Then trading commenced on the open market. When that happens, you see two prices: a bid price and an ask price (sometimes the

---

[16] I generally prefer floats under 20 million, and even under 10, but will sometimes consider 50 million, and never over 100 million.

ask price is called the offer price). The bid price is the highest price a buyer on a particular exchange is willing to pay. It's like bidding on something you want to buy on eBay. The ask price is the lowest amount that one or more sellers will accept for some shares.

It's super important to keep in mind one thing: these shares are being *auctioned off*. In the 1700s when the New York Stock Exchange started, you had a bunch of men in top hats down on Wall Street in New York City, auctioning off shares of stock the way they might auction a bale of hay. If people really need hay, it goes to the highest bidder. If there is too much hay available, the price drops because buyers can take their time and negotiate lower prices.

It feels like we live on another planet these days, with all our technology, but the auction principle is the same in stock markets. In our new company, after the shares initially were purchased at $10, then the bid price moved up to $11.57 because there were more buyers than sellers. The ask price was a bit higher, at $11.77.

Understanding spreads

The twenty-cent difference between the bid price and the ask price is called the *spread*. Some stocks trade with a 1-cent spread, and other stocks trade with 25-50 cent spreads or more. Minimum spreads are regulated by exchanges. The rule states that stocks priced over $1.00 must be quoted in increments of no less than 1 cent. That means the smallest spread you would see on a stock over $1.00 would look like $10.05 x $10.06.

For stocks under $1.00, exchanges allow quotes down to the 1/100th of a penny. You could therefore see a quote look like this: .0001 x .0002 for the lowest-price stock on the entire market. That right there is the bottom of the barrel.

What's interesting about this is that for a stock to move from 90 cents to $1.00, it's only ten cents. However, since sub-$1.00 stocks can be priced by the 1/100th of a penny, in theory it could take 1,000 increments if the stock began trading at .9000 and slowly moved up to .9999 before breaking $1.00. Then to go from $1.00 to $1.10 is only ten increments. This is why active traders will notice a phenomenon where stocks can move slowly when they are 85 or 95 cents a share, but as soon as they cross $1.00 they can move much faster.

As you know, I rarely trade stocks under $1.00, and the price quote is one reason. The 1/100th of a penny spreads are too tight. So what exactly does the spread tell us? A tight spread indicates a higher volume battle between buyers and sellers and is typically associated with consolidation and periods of lower volatility.

A wide spread typically reflects low participation of buyers and sellers. This can occur on both large-cap stocks and small-caps. If a stock has a wide spread with no volume, there will be no volatility. However, if a stock with a wide spread has breaking news, the wide spread combined with *higher relative volume* can actually fuel volatility.

The important thing to highlight is the difference between high average volume, and high relative volume.

Many large-cap stocks have higher levels of daily volume than small caps, simply because of large investment funds, mutual funds, and individual investors buying and selling those shares. This increase in average daily volume creates tight, or narrow, spreads.

To profit from the frequent buyers and sellers, large institutional investors become registered to serve as market makers. This is a business of arbitrage.

Market makers serve as middlemen, much like the auctioneers in the 1700s on Wall Street. They buy from somebody who is selling, and resell the same shares to somebody who is buying. They profit from the spread of the stock, and thus have an incentive to keep spreads larger. Competition among market makers—combined with higher participation from traders—create tighter spreads. The competitive market making that creates tight spreads will be far more present on stocks that have both **high average daily volume** and **low average daily volatility.**

Market makers carry the risk that while they are holding a stock, bad news could come out that creates volatility. Certainly some stocks are more prone to this happening (small-cap stocks), while others are considered more stable, like large caps. Thus, the best opportunity for market makers to generate consistent daily profits with minimal risk is to focus on stocks with higher average volume and lower average volatility.

Today, market making has become automated through high-frequency trading algorithms. These algorithms can adapt to changes in the market. They provide tremendous liquidity by placing orders on the bid and the ask when stocks have low volatility. But when stocks experience heightened volatility, the algorithms turn off: market makers close up shop to manage their risk. This is when day traders can step in to capitalize on volatility without competing against the institutional traders.

When I'm trading, I don't love to see a stock with a 1-cent spread, nor do I like to see a stock with a 50-cent spread. There is a sweet spot.

More than anything else, what I look for is a fast rate of change. I want to see a stock moving up quickly. Once a stock is moving over 10 percent on the day—and certainly if it's trading more than 5-10 percent in the last 10-15 minutes—we will see algorithms turn off and volatility spike. Spreads may get bigger, perhaps 10-15 cents on a stock under $20, but that's perfectly okay with me. Once the stock comes back into a period of consolidation, the market will seem to fill back in with orders as market makers resume their positions on the bid and the ask.

Volatility and liquidity

You will hear me say more than once in this book that I'm a hunter of volatility. I hunt for stocks where the price is changing quite a lot at the moment. I also look for stocks where the rate of change is happening with many shares changing hands, **relative to the normal activity of that stock**. This is what creates the high relative volume.

However, if a stock has an average volume of only 100 shares a day, and then today trades with 10,000 shares of volume, although it does have a relative volume ratio of 100:1, there may not be enough liquidity to buy and sell the stock. Liquidity comes in the form of market makers posting orders to buy and sell shares, as well as individual investors placing orders. If a stock has few orders, it will have wide spreads, and although it could move quickly with news, big moves on low liquidity stocks can be especially difficult to trade.

Just as with spreads, there is a sweet spot when it comes to relative volume, total volume, and liquidity. And no two trades or stocks are exactly the same.

As the owners of our publicly traded ice cream company, our goal is to expand the company, increase public awareness of our brand, and as a result see the value of the company grow. This should be reflected in the share price. Because we don't pay dividends but reinvest profits to fuel further growth, the only reason a shareholder will be comfortable holding shares is if the share price is steady or moving up. We must exceed our earnings expectations and continue to paint a picture of how even more valuable the company will be in the future.

As owners of this company, we couldn't care less about day traders. Through our quarterly and annual filings, we tell shareholders and prospective investors how we are doing. We also have the chance to issue press releases to announce exciting news. Publicly traded companies have an investor-relations department that not only does regulatory filings but also handles publicity and news releases.

Day traders are often among the first people to pick up on news released by a company. I view these press releases with a certain skepticism. Companies naturally will try to paint themselves in the most flattering way. When news first hits the news feeds, high-frequency trading algorithms are typically the first to execute trades. They are programmed to read headlines and execute trades based on certain keywords. Keywords like "buyout," "merger," or "contract with Apple" can all trigger what is called an *algo spike*. This is when algorithms initiate buy orders, and on a low volume stock, this sudden surge of volume can trigger market makers to pull back their orders. Within minutes the price of a stock can skyrocket. This is great news for day traders, and it's great news for the company, too.

Ultimately, the substance of the news headline does matter. Over the course of hours, and certainly over days and weeks, the market will begin to align with the correct value of the company. However, in the moments when news is breaking, and during periods of heightened volatility, stocks can become very disconnected from their true market value.

As an example, we put out news that our ice cream company brought a former Walmart executive onto our board of directors to get our brand on their shelves. Could the stock price surge from $10 a share to $20 a share in a single day? If the float of our stock is less than 50 million shares, it's not unthinkable.

That's how a company can double in value virtually overnight. Over the following few weeks, it's possible that analysts, market commentators and traders will begin to think the company could become huge. In that case the price could continue to rise, all the way to $50 a share, or five times its value prior to the news.

Let's say that for a variety of reasons an agreement doesn't materialize, and our ice cream never makes its way onto Walmart's shelves. It means that for a period, our share price was very disconnected from the true value of the company. It is not the current value of a company that creates its stock market price. Traders and market participants buy up a stock based on the perceived future value of that company.

As day traders, our job is to hunt for such volatility, because that is where we'll find opportunity.

Margin

When you first open a brokerage account, you'll notice an option to apply for margin or to open a cash account. A margin account allows you to do a couple of things you can't do in a cash account. The first is that it allows you to leverage your account and borrow money on margin (credit) from your broker, in order to buy more stock.

Brokers in the United States offer 4x intraday leverage and 2x overnight leverage. That means with a $25,000 account, you can day trade with up to $100,000. That's risky! It means if you bought 10,000 shares of a $10 stock, worth $100,000, and it went up 10 percent, you'd have a profit of $10,000. That's a 40 percent return, unless it lost 10 percent, in which case it's a 40 percent loss.

Buying on margin is an asymmetric results-magnifier: you can multiply your profits, which is nice. Then again, margin has the potential to wipe you out. This risk of blowing up an account is not worth the benefit of making more on a winner. That you, as a beginner, will be offered a margin account by your broker should not be interpreted as a recommendation to trade on margin. Your first order of business is to manage your risk.

— GUARDRAIL #3 —

In retrospect, I would not trade on margin until I've proven that I can make money consistently using my own cash.

By "consistently", I mean at least 6-12 months of profitability. I also need to have experienced drawdowns and recovered from them. More on drawdowns later.

The long and short of it

Money begets creativity. Ever since the stock exchanges began, there have been people with ideas about how to make trading more sophisticated, more complex, or more confusing—depending on how you look at it. Take the concept of short selling, for example. When someone buys stock in our new ice cream company, that person has "gone long" or "taken a long position" as we say. You buy a stock at what you hope is a lower price, own it, and then sell it at some point for hopefully a higher price.

But there's an opposite way to do it: you borrow stock from someone else, sell the stock, and then buy it back later. "Huh?" you ask. That's right: you don't own the stock, but someone else does. You borrow shares from them, and pay them a fee for their shares, then you sell those shares at what you think is a high price for the stock. You plan to buy back the shares at a lower price, and return them to the original owner. Your profit (or loss) is the difference between the price you sold shares at, and the price you bought them back at, not counting fees.

Short selling is a big business. Not as big as being long, but still many people are short sellers. They're the famous stock market "bears" who think things will soon go to hell, or they might just think that one stock is overvalued. It's also why some people will trash a stock in television interviews, on social media, or in chat rooms, because they're literally invested in seeing that stock go down.

The topic of short selling is involved, so I won't get into the details here, except to say:

── GUARDRAIL #4 ──

I would have avoided shorting stocks with real money until I established a profitable track record of trading in a simulator for at least 3-6 months.

You have a whole career ahead of you, where you can make money—and lose money—in all sorts of interesting ways in the market. The reason to stay away now is simply this: If you're "long a position" and you bought shares at a cost of $5,000, then the most you can lose is $5,000. If you sold short for $5,000, you might lose multiples of

"Short selling is why some people will trash a stock in television interviews, on social media, or in chat rooms, because they're literally invested in seeing that stock go down."

$5,000. And it can happen in *minutes*.

I've seen a stock go from $20 a share to over $2,500 a share in under a week. This could turn an initial 400-share short position valued at $8,000 to a staggering loss of $1,000,000. Of course, inversely this stock provided tremendous opportunities for traders who bought the stock while it was increasing in price and who followed their strategy and knew when to take profit off the table before overstaying their welcome.

When you're first learning to juggle, I suggest you start out with soft beanbags, and not running chainsaws.

———■———

Now that we've covered some foundational definitions, let's move on to the next layer of what you need to know in this business.

CHAPTER 7

The Battle That Will Happen Between Your Ears

I DON'T WANT TO BE OVERLY DRAMATIC when I say that a battle will soon happen between your ears if you choose to day trade. On the one hand, you're not going into real combat. But what I see too often on social media is a casual approach to day trading, as if it's a hobby like gardening. I was reading about a guy who bragged that he traded on his phone at stop lights. While driving for Uber. He might be trading, and he might even be day trading, where he closes out all of his positions before the end of the day. But he is by no means what I would call a true day trader.

To be a true day trader, you need to work hard to put several things in place:

- You must understand the terminology and how markets work. This book is a solid introduction to that knowledge, but there's always more to learn.
- You need certain equipment and assets; for example, you need a brokerage account to trade in, the appropriate equipment, and at least minimum funding of your account. We've covered that already.
- You must understand how very risky day trading is. The chances of succeeding long term are severely stacked against you—unless you take every opportunity to reduce those risks. We'll discuss how, in a moment.

Another way to say it is you need to stand on someone's shoulders and internalize a whole lot of principles.

What I want to emphasize here is that it's not only vital that you have a support system when you trade; you must also study hard to learn and use a set of principles that are worth their weight in gold. If you follow these principles that are hard won from people who came before you, it's *possible* that day trading could be for you. If you don't follow them, it's almost certain that you will be ground up and unceremoniously spit out of this business, and in surprisingly short order.

The first set of principles relate to your noggin: what's in there that should not be, and what you need to install into it.

> "...it's not only vital that you have a support system when you trade; you must also study hard to learn and use a set of principles that are worth their weight in gold."

Taking out the trash

Carefully curate what you put in your head. You don't need to look far to see mountains of junk, in the form of social-media trash talking. It's bad enough to hear the normal stuff on social media about politics, celebrities, and so forth. That kind of endless chatter is just a big harmless waste of time. But when you get your information about day trading from social media, now you're playing with fire.

Day trading is difficult enough on its own; every moment you must be focused on separating the signal from the noise: what's happening, what it means, when you detect a pattern, and what to ignore. Do not add the noise of social media to that significant cognitive load.

Be very careful whom you tell that you're day trading. Ignoring this single bit of advice can ruin your trading career before it ever gets off the ground. In Chapter 3 I discussed some myths surrounding day trading. Most of the people you know will believe those myths, and more:

- "You're doing *what*? Don't you know that it's pure gambling? Don't you know that you'll lose your shirt?"
- "Bless your heart, but you've never been good with numbers. What makes you think *you* will be able to day trade?"
- "If that was a sound way to make money, why wouldn't Warren Buffett and Elon Musk be doing it?"
- "I know a guy who lost his house and his wife divorced him, all based on his day trading losses."
- "Don't you remember when Cousin Ralph tried it and he lost his ass? And *he* went to MIT! If it didn't work for

Ralph, it sure as hell will not work for you!"

When you're just starting out in day trading, even a well-meaning comment from a loved one can mess with your head. When you announce to the world that you are a day trader, you create expectations for yourself and for others to measure you by. You'll have plenty of time down the road to tell others what you do, if you stick with it. But for now, I suggest you tell as few people as possible. Keep your circle small, preferably consisting of people who can be supportive as you're learning.

Focus more on the risk you need to manage, instead of the return you'd like to have. You most likely already know that day trading *can* be profitable, or you would not have picked up this book in the first place. The type of investors who buy and hold for the longer term will typically look for 5-10 percent annual returns. Contrast that with day traders, who are looking for trades that have the potential to make 5-10 percent returns *in a single day*. That kind of return comes with very high corresponding risk, but some day traders don't stop there: they'll trade on margin. In Chapter 6 we discussed the risk of using margin and leverage. It has the power to amplify gains and losses by a power of x4.

"...it takes great skill and dedication to realize that upside. It takes no skill at all to be the owner of the downside."

It's true that profits are potentially available for traders who work hard to learn the craft. The only little problem is that it takes great skill and dedication to realize that upside. It takes no skill at all to be the owner of the downside.

Your next tattoo

The whole purpose of this book is to paint a truthful picture of how day trading really works, and what it will really take for you to become a good trader. Then you can decide if it fits with your situation.

Books are long and it's hard to remember most of what's in them. I therefore want to hand you a big, shiny nugget:

A day trader is a hunter of volatility and a manager of risk.

Think about getting that tattooed somewhere. If you're sound asleep on a commuter train and somebody shakes you awake, saying, "Who are you?" your automatic answer should be: "Um, I'm a hunter of volatility and a manager of risk."

We'll talk much more in the next chapter about the volatility part, but let's first examine risk management.

How you measure a trade before you take it

When professional day traders look at a possible trade, they describe it in a very particular way. It is not using adjectives like "amazing" or "epic," though some of them may brag that way later, over a beer. Instead they describe the trade in terms of expected profit potential and acceptable downside risk.

"A day trader is a hunter of volatility and a manager of risk."

Let's take a stock that's selling for $10 per share. I'm thinking about trading 100 shares. Based on my analysis of where that stock has been trading recently, and where it is right now, I think my next trade has the potential to go up $1.00 per share. When I take the trade, I don't want to stay in it if the stock drops $0.50 or more from my entry point. This plan could be expressed in three ways:

- **On a per-share basis,** it's buying at $10.00 with a target profit of $11.00 and a maximum acceptable loss at $9.50.
- **For the trade of 100 shares,** I could say that I'm buying in with $1,000, and my target profit is $100, while my maximum acceptable loss is $50.
- **If we want to look at ratios,** then it's expressed as target profit, divided by acceptable loss. That means $100 / $50, or 2:1.

They are all the same trade, but expressed differently. You'll come across each of these ways of describing a trade, so it's good to be familiar with them.

"But Ross, how can you be so sure of the profit potential and the acceptable loss amount? You haven't made the trade yet! Where's your crystal ball?"

Fair question. I'm still searching for that crystal ball, but until I find one, I need to use the next best thing: I must rely on day trading principles and knowledge in general, and the trading history of the stock in particular. I call this educated intuition.

The upside measurement of $100 in the example above should never be what I merely *hope* is going to happen. It has to be based on a defensible and rational expectation. However, the downside of $50 should indeed be a firm number, as you'll see in a moment.

Now that we can describe trades, let's look at a typical situation:

Imagine a trader who has just made nine trades. In each trade, there was a $100 profit potential and a $50 acceptable risk. Therefore, each trade had upside potential that was double the downside risk, for a 2:1 profit/loss ratio.

Those first nine successful trades produced $900 in total profit, because our trader got out at the target amount. Good going! (Later, we'll discuss why and how you should let your winners keep winning, but for now, let's stick with the example.)

On the tenth trade, our trader found himself down $50 pretty quickly. But the day's gone so well! Instead of accepting the loss, the untrained trader purchased more shares at a lower price. After all, that's good investing, right? He's dropped his average cost, because he bought some stock at $10 and more at $9 for an average cost of $9.50 per share. That's good, right?

Things moved quickly, and the trader continued to hope that the stock would rebound at any second—except it didn't. Hope is not a trading strategy. The trader finally took the loss when he was down $1,000.

On paper, this trader had a 90 percent success rate today! Nine out of ten trades were positive. That's not bad, right? Except the trader is down $100 for the day. ($900 profit from the first nine trades, against a $1,000 loss.) He failed to manage his risk.

How to become a world-class loser

Over my many years as a trader and also as a leader of a trading community, I have heard from literally thousands of traders and aspiring traders. Most experienced a devastating loss at some point, because of avoidable mistakes. Unforced errors.

Some of them went downhill spectacularly quickly, because they traded on margin. Brokerage firms provide useful services, but one of them is not being your trading chaperone, making sure you don't get into trouble. The money to trade on margin is a few mouse clicks away, and the allure of quick profits can lead to new—and even seasoned—traders to ignore what they *know*, in favor of what they *feel* at the moment.

The small number of traders who consistently profit from the market have one skill in common: they cap their losses. They are world-class losers.

Who would want to be such a thing? You should want it, because in your trading career you *definitely will* do a lot of losing. On a really good day, you will win more than you lose, and will end the day with a net profit. But I can assure you—with tens of thousands of trades under my belt—that even on those good days, you will have at least a few losing trades. Becoming really good at handling loss can mean the difference between prospering in this business, and washing out.

Successful traders accept that each trade should have a *predetermined* level of risk. They articulate that risk level ahead of the trade, and then they adhere to the rules they set for the trade. It's that simple, and it's a critical part of a well-defined trading strategy.

Compare that to the untrained, shoot-from-the-hip trader. He wants to "stay flexible" so he adjusts his risk parameters mid-trade to accommodate a losing position. After all, he set his sell level at -$50, but the trade went down to -$60. He then thought that he'll hold on for "just a few more minutes" to see if it comes back up. Before he knows it, he's looking at an $80-100 loss, or worse, and he wonders how it happened. Ask me how I know this.

I'll be the first to admit that it's extremely difficult to maintain the level of discipline needed to sell when you hit your max loss on a trade. Nobody wants to lose, but the best traders know it's part of the business. If a salesperson freaked out every time she struck out and didn't make a sale, she wouldn't be in sales long. The sales pro follows a system and knows the statistics: after a string of rejections, a sale is statistically just around the corner.

> "The small number of traders who consistently profit from the market have one skill in common: they cap their losses. They are world-class losers."

It's also worth reminding yourself that losses shouldn't be considered mistakes. A mistake is when you break the rules of your strategy. A loss is simply when a trade based on your strategy didn't work as expected. You stopped at the correct price required to maintain a healthy profit-to-loss ratio on your trades for the day; in other words, you took the proper actions.

Dedicated day traders accept their losses without beating themselves up, and move on to the next trade. They **never allow** one trade to destroy their account or their career. This characteristic helps to keep them in the business as a member of the select club of long-term survivors.

> "...losses shouldn't be considered mistakes. A mistake is when you break the rules of your strategy. A loss is simply when a trade based on your strategy didn't work as expected."

Lifelong valuable skill to learn: mindfulness

The skill to take losses and not allow them to cause you to lose focus is an act of mindfulness. In our popular culture, mindfulness is usually confused with meditation, but they are not the same. Mindfulness has nothing to do with sitting in a certain pose, with your eyes closed in a calm setting, holding your fingers in a certain way. You can be mindful while running flat out, or while intently looking at your stock-trading screens. Mindfulness is a way of stepping back mentally, and observing what your own brain is doing at the moment. I highly recommend that you explore this technique. One way to do it is to get a book by Jon Kabat-Zinn called *Wherever You Go There You Are.*[17]

Our human emotions often work against us while we are in the thick of a trade. The emotions of fear and greed are present in every trader, including me. The very best traders can *experience those emotions without acting on them.* When you allow your emotions to overtake your rational thought process, you risk over-trading, exposing yourself to unnecessary risk and excessive losses.

At least in my experience, it takes years of emotional conditioning to be able to sit for even two hours, watching the live trading action while maintaining emotional composure the whole time. But when

---

[17] https://www.amazon.com/Wherever-You-There-Are-Mindfulness/dp/1567319920/

you can do this, you will have reached a new level of mastery over your emotions. This composure during a stressful situation will carry over into the rest of your life. If you can be a day trader with big money on the line and keep your composure? Well, the run-of-the-mill daily frustrations will also become easier for you to handle.

We're not quite done with exploring the forces at work in your head when you trade. We must confront a pair of four-letter words that will have a lot to do with whether you sink or swim as a day trader.

CHAPTER 8

Risk and Fear in Trading

SOME THINGS CANNOT BE SEPARATED: two sides of a coin is one example. Another is the experience of risk and fear in day trading.

This isn't shaping up to be much of a rah-rah book about trading, is it? It would be more fun to talk about huge profits instead of fear and risk, but that wouldn't be doing you a service. We're going to look both of these concepts in the eye. We'll not be able to eliminate risk and fear, but we sure can take specific steps to reduce both of them.

Profit/loss ratios in more detail

In the last chapter I introduced you to the crucial concept of the profit/loss ratio. This is another example of what should be inseparable but is not to most inexperienced traders: you should never even consider taking a trade where you have only focused on the upside and have not set the number where you will sell if things go south. Maybe the "path of least resistance" is to trade with your gut instincts because things are moving fast and you don't have time to set your loss number. Don't take that path.

I am not dismissing intuition; I'm saying that beginning traders need to follow best practices more than anyone, because they don't have the experience and bankroll to be wrong too many times. Taking away the safety net is no way to learn the trapeze.

I have both the experience and the bankroll to go with my gut, but even so, I set my max loss number before I trade. And I can't tell you how many times it's saved my butt.

In the last chapter we looked at the example of a stock and where we would set our maximum acceptable loss and profit target. Let's put the trade in graphical terms, because that will make it easier to understand another important calculation. I am going to use a stock price that I normally don't trade, just so the math is extremely clear.

Let's say we have a stock trading at $30. Based on experience and the stock's current behavior, my target profit for the stock is $40. In real life I probably wouldn't have a max loss 33 percent away from the current price, but for the sake of this example, let's stick with it. My maximum acceptable loss is $20. You can see this example in Column B in Figure 8-1:

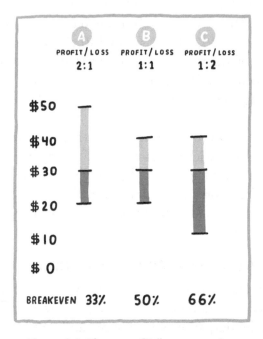

Figure 8-1: Three profit/loss scenarios

In Chapter 7 we looked at the example of a trader who had a success rate of 90 percent over ten trades, but still lost money. He didn't establish and stick to his maximum acceptable loss in just one trade, and that killed his day.

Remember that success rate is how often you were green (profitable). Now look at Figure 8-1 again, but with Success Rate in mind. You can see that our entry point of $30 is halfway up the bar in Column B. We stand to gain the exact amount we are willing to risk. This is called a 1:1 profit/loss ratio, and it requires 50 percent accuracy to be breakeven.

"But Ross, what if all my losing trades lost by $9.00 but all my winning trades won by only $1.00? Couldn't I be overall red and still have a success rate over 50 percent?"

Yes you could. And in fact, if you ignore the maximum acceptable loss and ride those red trades down, you'll quickly kill your overall results. But I'm assuming, for the point that I'm about to make, that there is a random distribution of results. If you're green on fifty or more of those trades, you'll be green overall.

Okay, so let's look at Column C. Here we set our maximum acceptable loss at $10, which is $20 below our entry point of $30, and our target profit is $40, which is only $10 above our entry. That is a profit/loss ratio of 1:2, which we call "inverted" or "negative." In order for us to be green overall, we need to be right 66 percent of the time. We are allowing the stock to go down twice as far as we hope for it to go up.

Conversely, we have Column A. In this case, we will take this trade only if we see twice as much upside as we will allow for downside. That is a 2:1 profit/loss ratio. We only need to be right 33 percent of the time to be at breakeven. However, I'll say as a day trader that it's easier said than done to find trades where your profit potential is multiples of your risk.

These two numbers tell me a lot about a trader

Profit/loss ratios are often overlooked by novice traders, who maybe don't appreciate the probabilities we just covered. But remember, at the end of the day, success or failure can be viewed simply in the metrics of your trades.

GUARDRAIL #5

I generally look for trades with a minimum 2:1 profit/loss ratio.

Traders are eternally optimistic, and so if you think something has 2:1 profit/loss potential, you're likely to walk away a little short. But that's okay! Just factor that in by aiming a little higher. The reality is that you can control your downside, but the upside profit target and whether it's obtainable is an educated guess. Those guesses typically get better with experience. That's the "educated intuition" I referred to earlier. So aim high with a 2:1 profit/loss target, but make sure you can maintain a minimum ratio of 1:1. In that case, you can break even while being right just 50 percent of the time.

The first thing I tell traders to look at is their trade history. All traders should know their profit/loss ratios and their success rate. These numbers will indicate whether a strategy is sustainable. If you can trade with a 1:1 or even a 2:1 profit/loss ratio, it becomes much easier to succeed.

> **"If you can trade with a 1:1 or even a 2:1 profit/loss ratio, it becomes much easier to succeed."**

Of course, to get a higher profit/loss ratio, you may need to be more selective. That means you may trade less frequently, as you patiently wait for an opportunity to achieve a 2:1 trade. It puts pressure on you, because you may even sit for an hour or two—or a whole trading session—and not see an opportunity that meets those criteria. That takes experience and discipline to pull off, because it can feel like you are not doing anything.

In major-league baseball, the new kids who just made the team may want to swing at each pitch, because they so badly want to prove their worth. The veterans know their strengths and weaknesses. They might know, for example, that their personal "sweet spot" is to wait for a fastball that's high and inside. They'll be patient, and will even be willing to look like they're not doing anything for most of the at-bat, or even the game. Then they see a pitch that's exactly where they want it, and they swing.

The veterans are not any stronger than the young bucks. They may even be physically weaker. But they have the experience and discipline to wait for a pitch that matches their criteria. They have the rare mental strength to lay off until they see their money pitch. And when they see it, they often connect. That's how you get into the Hall of Fame, and that's how you become a professional day trader.

> **"...no one gave them the mental conditioning necessary to wait...and wait....and wait some more, until that special circumstance presented itself to them."**

Most traders who fail will trade

with inverted profit/loss ratios like 1:2. This is also extremely common with beginner traders. Unfortunately, when you trade with a negative profit/loss ratio, you are in effect setting the bar too high. With an inverted ratio of 1:2, you must be right over 66 percent of the time to be profitable. That is an unsustainable strategy—especially for a rookie!

The sad truth is that the failed traders might permanently exit the market, having never realized that they were destined for failure because no one told them about the only types of pitches that they should swing at. Also, no one gave them the mental conditioning necessary to wait…and wait….and wait some more, until that special circumstance presented itself to them.

— GUARDRAIL #6 —

It's crucial—but not enough—for me to know my profit/loss ratio on a trade. I work hard to stick to those boundaries in the heat of trading. Changing risk parameters to accommodate a bad trade has not worked well in my experience.

Cultivate discipline

A powerful way to reduce your trading risk is hidden in plain sight, because we've all heard about it for years—it's discipline.

In our trading courses, we spend a great deal of time stressing the importance of discipline. Many traders found us after taking other trading courses and finding themselves stuck in a cycle of poor trading habits, trading losses, and disappointment.

Having the knowledge of fundamental trading concepts is vital, but not enough. You must also think and act like a successful trader. This means selling losers quickly and holding partial positions in your winners as long as possible.

In order to help our traders to improve their ability to be disciplined, we strongly urge them to do a minimum of thirty minutes of exercise and fifteen minutes of meditation every day. I use exercise and meditation to help train my mind to cope with the significant stress that accompanies day trading. By forcing myself to do these two things every day, I'm practicing discipline. But I didn't choose just any two random activities to practice daily discipline on: exercise and meditation help to keep me both mentally grounded and sharp.

When I am in a trade and must make a hard decision, I need to fight the urge to sell the winners too soon and hold the losers too long. By practicing discipline in other areas of my life, I strengthen that muscle memory and improve my ability to maintain composure while trading.

Practicing discipline has another benefit: it's a way to condition my mind to become accustomed to the feeling of discomfort. Both risk and fear generate discomfort. Rather than look for ways to ignore or skirt around that feeling, I regularly work to train myself to withstand it and make sound decisions, even during that discomfort.

Many of the successful traders I know have strict exercise regimens because it helps their trading performance. The whole point is not to deny or block out the emotions of the moment—that is impossible. Instead, it's to recognize those emotions, and allow them to exist without acting rashly on those feelings. We'll talk more about it in Chapter 11, but one big benefit of journaling is that it helps you to develop an awareness of the stress you feel while trading, and to what degree it went beyond feelings and affected your actions in a trading session.

> "Practicing discipline has another benefit: it's a way to condition my mind to become accustomed to the feeling of."

It's called "practicing" discipline for a reason—it never ends. You might learn how to ride a bike, or swim, and when you come back to it years later, you still may have the knack. Discipline is much more like a muscle that you strengthen by exercising it regularly. If you ignore that muscle, it will weaken and eventually atrophy.

Even after years of trading, I still find myself occasionally giving in to my instinct to chase a stock for fear of missing the move, to sell a winner too soon, or hold a loser a little too long. *Every day* when I trade, I must fight against my natural instincts. Perhaps a few traders have a natural aptitude for the mindset required to be profitable, but I believe most of us have to really work at it.

It took me years to become successful. Looking back, I have realized that it was because of the emotional obstacles that stood in my way. I had a solid understanding of stocks, chart patterns, and trading strategies, but I kept falling into the cycle of big losers and small winners. It took a long time before I developed the self-awareness to realize what was causing those actions.

— GUARDRAIL #7 —

To maximize my ability to make the right decisions under stress, I try to exercise and meditate every day. It's one of the best ways to keep my discipline muscle strong.

Different types of risk

We've discussed the measurement of risk, in terms of the profit/loss ratio and success rate. We've also looked at how you can reduce risk by cultivating discipline and sticking with the profit/loss parameters you set before you make a trade. Now let's look at different types of risk, and how to deal with them.

Entry/stop risk. This is the distance between our entry point in the trade and our stop (or stop loss), which is shorthand for our maximum acceptable loss. If you look back at Figure 8-1, our entry point was $30 in each case, but we had different stops.

Your stop loss should be based not on a hunch, but on a recent support or resistance area. The detailed explanation of support and resistance is beyond the scope of this book, but these are prices that sometimes act like boundaries.

Volatility risk. This is the second type of risk that we need to be mindful of. I said in Chapter 7 that day traders are hunters of volatility and managers of risk. Not only do we want to see volatility, we should not trade without it, because it's volatility that presents opportunities to trade quickly and for prices to swing significantly.

We do love volatility, but only up to a point: extremely volatile markets can cause larger losses than we originally planned for. Breaking news has the potential to cause individual stocks or even the market at large to trade in extreme ranges. Instead of jumping into the market at such times, it's prudent to wait for the dust to settle before determining a potential trade opportunity.

Exposure risk. There are three elements to a trader's exposure: share price, the number of shares you are holding, and how long you hold them for. It's also called the value of the position.

Let's say I'm trading 1,000 shares of a stock that costs $10 per share, and I hold that position for ten minutes. I am not suggesting that we multiply 1,000 x 10 x 10 to get 100,000 of something. Instead, I use it as a rough sense of magnitude when comparing different trades.

Another aspect of exposure is what percentage of your portfolio is allocated to a stock. A longer-term investor typically will not allocate more than 10 percent to any single stock. Contrast that with day traders, who may allocate most or even all of their account's buying power to one stock at a time. Then again, day traders can mitigate that risk by holding shares for perhaps minutes, while investors sometimes hold positions for months or years.

Stock halts. This risk can be a nightmare for day traders with large positions. The exchanges can halt trading at any time, and for a variety of reasons. There are market-wide halts that happen when some technical glitch or high-frequency trading algorithm goes haywire. These halts are rare, and may last for a few minutes, or can stretch to hours or even longer.

The more common stock halts are because of volatility or pending the release of material news. Volatility halts are sometimes called "circuit breaker" halts. If a stock rises or falls over 10 percent in a five-minute period, the stock will be halted automatically for five minutes. This volatility pause gives traders a chance to analyze news, get their bearings, and slow down. When markets are volatile overall, this type of halt is common. Often it will be because of some news leaking about a company, or even a rumor, which causes a rapid enough move to trigger the halt.

Stock halts due to pending news is one of the greatest risks in trading. Stocks susceptible to being halted pending news include stocks surging up rapidly for no apparent reason. In this case, it is not uncommon for the company to issue a statement regarding the price action or to address the rumors that may be causing the price action. Although stocks can be halted at any time pending news, typically the news is released when the market is closed.

Another type of stock halt that can happen on any stock, but that is more common with penny stocks, is a "T12" halt. It happens when the exchange requests additional information from the company. This type of halt can last for weeks or even months, and is often related to a pending government investigation. Because penny stocks are sometimes used for market manipulation and fraud, a penny stock that goes up 500 percent on no news could be at risk of being halted either pending news or on a T12. This is one reason why I avoid trading penny stocks.

As day traders, we have to be mindful of the potential for stock halts and limit our positions on stocks that are at risk of being halted. Penny stocks are one example of this; also be careful with stocks trading on news that has not been released or confirmed by the company itself.

> "As day traders, we have to be mindful of the potential for stock halts and limit our positions on stocks that are at risk of being halted."

Stock halts are another reason trading on margin can be so dangerous. If you were trading on margin and got caught in a stock halt, if that stock opens down 20 percent, it could cause a loss for you that's somewhere between massive and catastrophic.

The problem is that any time a stock is halted, it can reopen at a much-different price. The risk is that a stock could reopen far below your maximum acceptable loss amount. The reason a stock can open higher or lower is that while the stock is halted, buy orders and sell orders change in response to the news or volatility. If a stock is going up, sellers may pull their orders, while new buyers place orders to get in higher. This creates an imbalance. If there are more buyers, the price will open higher. If there are more sellers, the price will open lower.

Typically, stocks that halt while going up will then open higher, and stocks that halt while going down will later open lower. However, with a halt on a T12 review, I've never seen a stock open higher. With a halt on pending news, the resumption will be based on market reaction to the news.

Becoming great at being wrong

In Chapter 7 I talked about the importance of being a good loser. In our current discussion about risk, I want to get more specific about loss in trading.

When I speak with a trader who recently experienced a large loss, the first thing I do is tell them to spend some time reviewing the trade that resulted in the loss. I always begin by asking the trader what their profit/loss ratio was when they entered the trade. Almost always I get one of the following responses:

- "What's a profit/loss ratio?" (Traders in my community know what it is, but I frequently speak with people who got their training elsewhere.)
- "I forgot to set my profit/loss ratio in my need to jump in."
- "I set a good one, Ross! But I can't believe how fast things went south, and I just kept holding."

We already talked about two guardrails I identified:
- I generally look for trades with a 2:1 profit/loss ratio potential, or better; and
- I work hard to stick to those numbers, regardless of what my emotions tell me at the time.

Just following those two rules has the potential to save all kinds of money and grief. But we can save even more by adding the following:

— GUARDRAIL #8 —

I set *and follow* a maximum loss amount per trade, and a maximum loss amount per day.

Setting a daily max loss to be the same as my daily profit target, yet another number to have, is another way to manage risk. I did not put the profit target in "guardrail" form because it is not as crucial as the max loss, though it's still important.

If I have a $200 daily profit target and I find myself down $200 on the day—I shut down my computer and walk away.

"But Ross, what if I'm super close to turning things around?

> "If you become one of those traders who frequently is down beyond their maximum acceptable loss, there is a solution: set automatic stop-loss orders with your broker."

What if things are looking promising so that I'm almost sure that I can make up some of that loss? After all, it worked that way for me last week. Blindly following rules should not trump judgment."

Yes they should. To put it more precisely, the judgment is in creating those rules. Although it is difficult to accept defeat, it's far more important to realize that once you have exceeded your max loss, your judgment is almost guaranteed to have been compromised. It is always best to walk away instead of attempting to trade in a compromised emotional state. Day traders don't have the luxury of taking time to "sleep on it" or to "grab some fresh air and think it over." The guardrails are built on the very places where people veer off the road without them.

About the max loss per trade, I typically set it at about 25 percent of my daily profit target. If I take a trade and the market suddenly turns against me, I take the loss. If I take three or four trades like that in a row, it's time to shut it down before things get worse. I've gotten better at reading the writing on the wall and walking away sooner.

Over many years of leading a trading community, I have found that some traders are very good at taking their losses, but others struggle to press the Sell button. Some even turn short-term day trades into long swing trades by not liquidating on the same day.

If you become one of those traders who frequently is down beyond their maximum acceptable loss, there is a solution: set automatic stop-loss orders with your broker. If the price falls below the stop trigger price, your order will automatically execute and you avoid having to press the Sell button yourself. Even though it's difficult to hand over this aspect of trade management to a computer, it can make a big difference for the account health for traders who struggle to take losses at the predetermined time.

This brings us to the next guardrail:

GUARDRAIL #9

Sometimes I ask my broker to set a max position size (both in shares and dollar value), and a max daily loss on my account.

I still use both to this day. I give myself breathing room, but this guardrail is there to protect me from a worst-case scenario. All sorts of things can happen, like: my toddler holding down the Buy button on my keyboard until I've maxed out my buying power, a sticky key from a malfunctioning keyboard, or a moment of compromised emotional judgment. Even as an experienced trader, I feel more comfortable trading knowing I have a safety net on my account. As my grandmother always said, it's better to be safe than sorry.

Using guardrails to protect against catastrophic losses is like an athlete trying to protect against injury. A sports injury not only ruins that day, but it can have long-lasting opportunity costs during your rehabilitation. A big trading loss can take a long time to recover from, both psychologically and financially.

> "When you are trading, it's important to remind yourself that regardless of how you traded yesterday, last week, or last month, today is a new day."

When you are trading, it's important to remind yourself that regardless of how you traded yesterday, last week, or last month, today is a new day: it's your opportunity to prove to yourself that you can follow the rules and stick to your trading plan. If you want to succeed as a trader, it is crucial that you can hold yourself to the rules of max loss per trade and max loss per day.

Emotional Hijack

Day trading is a career where you can make a catastrophic mistake, and then keep trading moments later. You could take a 30,000-share position, lose $15,000, and then do it again five more times in a row. In just one day and with a handful of trades, you could easily blow up your entire account. This is how quickly a trader can become a gambler.

Once you've crossed that line on any day, you've crossed a point of no return. You have become a victim of what I call "emotional hijack."

This happens when a trade triggers a fight-or-flight response. It's typically a big loss, though it could also be a big win. I've developed awareness of this phenomenon and I notice that, following a triggering trade, my heart will start pounding, my palms are clammy, and I start to get tunnel vision. In this moment my brain subtly shifts from reason and logic to emotional and reflexive responses.

I've become pretty good at knowing my triggers, and I can typically catch myself before crossing the point of no return. If I experience the onset of an emotional hijack, I know to shut off my computer and not look at the market for the rest of the day. If I keep trading while in this state, disaster is imminent. This is a state of mind where I will take trades that all logic and reason would have told me to avoid. Later, when I look back at the damage, I ask myself, *What was I thinking?!*

Therein lies the clue of what's really happening: I was in fact not thinking during those moments. I wasn't calm and rational. I was fully in a state of emotional response, the way my distant ancestor might have felt while running from a saber-toothed tiger. In my case, it wasn't fear of death but fear of loss that triggered this fight-or-flight response.

In these moments, traders are simply gambling in a desperate attempt to avoid accepting loss. Developing acceptance of loss through emotional conditioning is a critical part of scaling up any strategy. This is a process of experiencing small losses with no reaction and gradually scaling up the size of your trades until you can experience a loss that at one time might have been triggering. Your practice of discipline will also be crucial in your ability to pull yourself away from the computer at the earliest sign of an emotional hijack.

Regardless of how much work you've done to prepare yourself for trades that could be triggering, it's important to recognize that we are only human. This is why it's important to have a safety net. My safety net comes in the form of the max loss and max position sizes that I have my broker set as restrictions on my account.

In other careers like race-car driving, if you crash your car into the wall, you're done with the race. You'll have to wait until the next race.

The very nature of that type of activity gives you a period to reflect on the mistakes you made that resulted in the accident. Or take sports, where we've all seen images of athletes smashing their tennis racket or golf club, or pushing other players in a fit of rage. These are forms of emotional hijack, where the consequences are not good. They damage their reputation and can cause costly penalties.

> "... one day of emotional hijack could be career-ending, if you don't have a safety net in place, in the form of guardrails."

In day trading, we don't have the luxury of a built-in time-out period after we make a mistake. The ability to continue slamming those Buy and Sell keys can make the cost of emotional hijack astronomical. In fact, one day of emotional hijack could be career-ending, if you don't have a safety net in place, in the form of guardrails.

Balancing your risk

In Chapter 7 we looked at how it's possible to have a 90 percent success rate and still lose money. It was because the first 9 trades yielded $100 profit each, and the tenth was a $1,000 loss. That scenario not only points to the shortcomings of looking only at success rate, but it also is an example of unbalanced risk.

— GUARDRAIL #10 —

I never want to have one trade weighted so heavily with risk that it has the power to erase more than one or two previous winners.

It's true, even if that big final trade had the proper 2:1 profit/loss potential (risking $1,000 to make $2,000). It is a poor decision because the risk of that one trade far outweighs the average risk per trade.

Many traders, including me, will adjust our risk per trade throughout the day, based on our performance and to adapt to different market conditions. This is a common practice used to increase profits on days when trading is good; but it's also used to reduce losses on days when trading is difficult.

The trick is to adjust risk in smaller increments, so the impacts of winners or losers does not have a strong effect on my overall performance. For example, I may have set my max acceptable loss for my first six trades at $100. Based on the results of those trades, for the next trade I might increase the risk (max acceptable loss) to $150, or decrease it to $75. I would not make a drastic change to my risk parameters in the middle of a trading day.

Many beginner traders may actually experience a great day until they decide that they're on a hot streak and swing for the fences. They take a high-risk, unbalanced position on what they think is a perfect setup. If they lose on that high-risk trade, they may give back their entire profits from the day and go into the red.

This is a disappointing financial loss, but what's even worse is the loss of confidence and the effect that it has on your emotions. This can quickly escalate into a "revenge trading" cycle of increasing risk and larger and larger losses. To avoid this situation entirely, a trader must balance risk across all trades. If that final trade turns out to be a loser, it does not ruin your day or your psychological control over future trades.

Just as you can have a success rate of 90 percent for the day and end up red, the opposite can also happen: you can have a success rate of 40 percent or even lower, and be green. The different outcomes result from following the risk-reduction guardrails—or not.

Picking good stocks is important, as we'll see in Chapter 10. But it is not as important as managing your risk on every trade. You should focus foremost on your profit/loss ratio and max loss on each trade.

The many faces of fear in trading

Fear is a natural emotion, and we've all experienced the straightforward version of it. For example, an aggressive dog lunging at us will elicit a primal fear.

With day trading, it's different. When we're trading, to our primal brains things might seem calm: we're in a comfortable room, looking at a monitor, and sipping a latte with no angry animals in sight.

Appearances are deceiving, however. Experienced day traders are intimately familiar with the many manifestations of fear that accompany every trading session. Let's review them.

Holding losers too long

The most-obvious form is the fear of financial loss. Many beginner traders and most failed traders will experience the tendency to hold their losers too long. Fear of loss is directly behind this behavior. Why do traders hold losers too long? It's because a trade is not a loss until you hit the Sell button. There is always the chance—however remote—that the price could pop back up if you have not punched that Sell button. The fear of making the loss real keeps you in the trade: it makes you think about finding a way to turn the trade around instead of just acknowledging that it's a losing trade, taking the loss, and moving on to the next trade.

The reality is that small losses are not a big deal, but a trader in an emotional state does not think that way. Sometimes traders will make a bad trade worse not just by waiting, but by averaging down. In other words, they will add shares at a lower price which reduces their average cost basis. This typically results in even larger losses, when it is not part of a proven strategy that involves scaling in and out of trades by averaging.

I have worked with traders who set $200 as the max acceptable loss, and on a trade when they were down $200, instead of simply cutting the loss, they decided to add more shares in the belief that they could "trade out of the loss." In reality, these trades often end in losses of $1,000 or more.

In hindsight, it is easy to say that the right thing to do was to simply cut the loss at -$200 and follow the rules you made for yourself. Unfortunately, in the heat of the moment, emotions can easily take control and your rational thoughts and plans get thrown out the window.

The irony of this behavior is the action that was based on a fear of loss actually resulted in the trader taking larger losses than if he had simply followed the plan. The second-most-important skill for new traders to learn is to cap their losses. The most-important skill is to create and follow their trading plan, regardless of emotions at the moment.

Selling winners too soon

If you enter a trade that has a good profit potential and it fits into your trading strategy, the last thing you should want to do is sell that trade before it has had a chance to work. If you are up ten cents on a trade that has the potential to make fifty cents and there is no clear reason to sell it—but you sell anyway—you've given in to a common counterproductive impulse.

"The second-most-important skill for new traders to learn is to cap their losses. The most-important skill is to create and follow their trading plan, regardless of emotions at the moment."

Why do so many traders sell their winners too soon? It's because the fear of loss has guided their decisions again. It's the fear of the small winner turning into a loser that convinces us to sell the trade too soon. Just as a loser isn't real until you hit the Sell button, a winner isn't real until you've hit that Sell button and locked it up. In the short term, we feel happy to have locked up some profit, if even a small amount.

It's a bad habit to get into, because you're conditioning yourself into capping your winners. We must learn to do the exact opposite: cap our losers and let our winners run. Capping winners will reduce your profit/loss ratio, and requires very high accuracy in order to be profitable.

When you sell your winners too soon, you're setting the bar for success higher than it needs to be. I can recommend an excellent book to you, called *Quit* by Annie Duke.[18] She made millions as a poker player, and has written extensively about decision-making.

In that book, she talked about a study that was done about taxi drivers. They had a lot of data from almost 2,000 drivers in New York City, relating to when drivers picked up customers, how much the rides were worth, and many other details. What they discovered was that taxi drivers did not make good decisions about when to keep driving and when to call it quits for the day:

Instead of maximizing their driving time when fares were plentiful and minimizing their unproductive time, they were likely to quit early when there was a lot of demand for their services. When there were few

---

[18] Duke, A. (2022). Quit. Portfolio. https://amazon.com/Quit-Power-Knowing-When-Walk-ebook/dp/B09PTLY4BL/

fares, they'd work the full twelve hours, wearing themselves out driving around for little benefit.

The researchers asked drivers how they made the decision to keep driving or quit. It turns out that drivers set a daily goal for how much they wanted to earn. That number took over their decision-making: if they hit the number early in the day—great. They could call it a day. If business was terrible and they weren't near their number, they would gut it out and keep going. It gets better:

[The researchers] calculated that the drivers would make 15% more income if they worked the exact same number of hours but allocated those hours based on demand. In fact, if drivers just chose a heuristic that was random, like working the same number of hours each day regardless of conditions, they would make 8% more than they were with the strategy they were using.

Annie Duke's book and this taxi-driver study particularly resonated with me because the parallels are striking with day trading. To be a successful trader, you need to cap your losses as we discussed earlier. That means on a day when the market isn't hot, rather than grinding it out and fighting hard to hit your daily goal, walk away. The longer you grind it out, the more susceptible you become to decision fatigue. When the market isn't in your favor, it's simply not worth trying to fight against that headwind.

"...on a day when the market isn't hot, rather than grinding it out and fighting hard to hit your daily goal, walk away."

On the other hand, on a day when the market is hot, if you hit your daily goal in the first ten minutes of trading and walk away, it could mean leaving an incredible amount of profit on the table. Typically, on my top ten trading days each year I exceed my daily goal by at least four times. In other words, if my daily goal is $5,000, my top ten trading days are all in excess of $20,000 in profit.

In this example, if I stopped trading on each of those ten days when I hit my goal, I would be leaving $150,000 of profit on the table, and would have only $50,000 in profit vs $200,000. This is a significant difference!

In fact, my top ten trading days typically amount to over 20 percent of my yearly profit. There are 250 trading days each year, and yet just ten have the power to dramatically change my year. This means as traders move from beginner, to intermediate, and then to advanced, a critical skill they need to learn is how to throttle up in a hot market trading session and throttle down in a cold market trading session.

In studying my trades, I've also found that my best days tend to be clustered together. This is because the overall market is hot, and not just one stock. The same pattern is true with my worst days. These losses are typically clustered together as I find myself over-trading during a cold market. However, it's not uncommon for hot and cold days to be back to back during choppy markets. This means trading may throttle up and back down quickly from day to day in response to market conditions.

— GUARDRAIL #11 —

I trade the market I'm in, not the market I want to be in. I throttle up when it's hot, throttle down when it's cold, and do everything possible to minimize drawdown so that each day I come to the table confident and ready to perform at my best.

Growing up in New England, I've always been a big skier. Conditions in New England regularly are icy, wet, or mushy, and we rarely get good powder. Experienced skiers often will tune their skis to the conditions by applying different types of wax. If they're really dedicated, they may even use different skis to match the conditions.

This approach is not too different from tuning or adapting a proven strategy to various market conditions. Throttling up or down is a way of trading the market you're in.

Besides trading longer on a hot day and trading less on a cold day, I will adapt share size and position management to suit market conditions.

When it comes to share size, as we previously discussed, it's important to manage risk fairly evenly across a trading session. However, in a hotter market, it makes sense for me to scale up share size to trade at the upper range of my limit. Trading at the edge of my comfort zone during a hot market has been the best way for me to maximize the opportunities. After all, a hot market is not the time to be trading conservatively with small size relative to whatever is typical for you.

If I decide to expand the upper range of my share-size limit, I only do that through a gradual period of small increases. If I currently max out at 10,000 shares and want to move my upper limit to 15,000 shares, I may increase 1,000 shares a week on average until I reach 15,000. This allows time for me to acclimate to the larger losses that will come with bigger positions. If I'm able to get comfortable trading at 15,000 shares, then I can begin to work towards 20,000 shares.

However, at some point there will be the inevitable drawdown as the market cools off. This is when I may ease back down to 10,000 shares until things pick back up. The challenge here is going from 10,000 shares one day to 20,000 the next day as the market shifts from hot to cold quickly. This type of a large fluctuation in share size should be reserved for experienced traders. As we discussed earlier in the book, the risk here is that you have five or six great days of trading with 10,000 shares, then on the day you go up to 20,000 you take a loss that wipes out the previous week of progress.

Besides adjusting my share size to market conditions, I can adjust my position management. That is the approach you take to scale into and out of trades. Most beginner traders will have one entry and one exit. There is no scaling. As a trader gains experience, they will often experiment first with one entry and two exits. This is called "scaling out" of a position. Rather than selling the full position when your profit target is hit, you choose to sell half and keep the rest. At the same time, this is where a trader would move up their stop loss to protect a profit on the remaining position they're holding.

During a hot market, let's say I bought 5,000 shares of a stock at $10.00, with a target of $11.00. My stop would need to be $9.50 in order to have a 2:1 profit/loss ratio. If the stock goes up to $11, rather than sell the whole position, I may choose to sell just a quarter of the position, or I may hold the entire position until a clear exit indicator forms. If the stock ends up going to $12, $13 or $14, my gain will be substantially higher. The most conservative strategy that most beginners will follow is to sell the whole position. That's safe, and there's nothing wrong with taking profit. Though it's not the optimal way to trade in a hot market, a beginner trader isn't going for peak performance yet. They are just trying to keep their head above water and maintain consistency.

In a cold market, I will be much more likely to sell the full position or take half off the table when I hit my profit target, rather than risk losing those gains. The more I see stocks failing to exceed my profit target, the more likely I'll be to sell sooner. On the other hand, when I repeatedly see stocks outperforming my price targets, I'll start to hold longer.

Market strength and sentiment becomes a bit of a self-fulfilling prophecy. If traders think the market is cold, they trade conservatively, thus keeping the market cold. If traders think the market is hot, they trade aggressively, thus keeping the market hot. Changes between hot and cold markets can happen quickly, as traders rush to adapt to the new environment.

The subtle changes in position sizing and position management in hot and cold markets can help maximize profits and minimize drawdown. Being able to adjust your strategy in real-time is the goal for any trader. This requires a deep connection both with the market and your awareness of your own emotional state. This is what we call "flow state" trading.

"But Ross, I thought you were all about what you said earlier: 'get green and shut it down.' Now it sounds like you're saying the opposite."

Good question! There's a right time for each approach. The "get green and shut it down" strategy is the way to go when:

- You're a beginner trader
- You're in a tight financial situation and cannot afford to make any mistakes
- You've recently experienced a big loss, or string of red days.

In all three cases, your emotions tend to run high, and your confidence is low. This is when your guardrails must be the narrowest.

Every day that you trade, you're doing one of two things: you're either leaving money on the table, or giving back profit. It hurts less to walk away with profit, knowing you left some money on the table, than it does to give back profit. In fact, I find if I give back more than half my profit on the day after hitting my daily goal, it can become a trigger for an emotional hijack.

As a beginner, it's super important to protect your emotional state. That state is similar to momentum: as you build consistency, you build confidence, and it's a positive feedback loop. However, one big loss can throw you off that positive feedback loop and send you right into a negative feedback loop of emotional hijack and poor trading decisions.

> "Every day that you trade, you're doing one of two things: you're either leaving money on the table, or giving back profit."

Experiencing a large drawdown has two costs. The first obvious cost is the money you lost in the trade. The less-obvious second cost is the opportunity cost during your period of trading with low confidence.

The safest way for a beginner to trade is by getting green and getting out. This isn't forever, but it's an important phase. You need this period of extreme discipline in order to build a track record of success. That track record becomes your source of confidence when you experience your first drawdown.

Once a beginner trader has recovered successfully from their first drawdown, they are ready to work on trading longer when the market is hot. This means confronting the risks that come with trading longer in the day, including decision fatigue and the risk of becoming emotionally triggered by giving back earlier gains. This is getting into intermediate and advanced day trading.

Sometimes I think of the guardrails as training wheels. They are an important tool for learning to trade safely that builds confidence and avoids bad experiences. Then again, you won't win the Tour de France with training wheels. At a certain point in your growth as a trader, you'll have the discipline and experience such that you can pull back many of the tightest guardrails. At that stage, you should have a level of emotional growth and self-awareness that you'll know when to walk away before a bad day gets out of hand.

> "...there's nothing wrong with a quick decision; in fact, it's important to be decisive. When you're quick to decide—and you don't follow your rules—that's when it can get expensive."

FOMO

A less-obvious form of fear is the fear of missing out on a big move in the markets. You may suddenly see a stock start to jump up on what might appear to be breaking news, or you see a technical indicator like a "reversal" taking shape. It's easy to feel inclined to jump into the market out of fear of missing a potential winner. That fear has guided your decision and led you into an unplanned trade.

You may then purchase at a price that's too far away from your stop, or take more shares than your risk tolerance allows. In seconds, you've made a decision and broken your rules. When these trades go badly, they often result in a larger loss than your strategy and rules allow for. When I speak with traders about a massive loss, they often say, "It happened so fast!"

In reviewing my own trading performance, my biggest losses were spontaneous trades I jumped into on an impulse. I saw the markets starting to move and jumped into a stock without fully analyzing my risk. When emotions guide your decisions, big mistakes are common. To be clear, there's nothing wrong with a quick decision; in fact, it's important to be decisive. When you're quick to decide—and you don't follow your rules—that's when it can get expensive.

Trader Rehab

This topic is not precisely a fear, but it's so wound up with emotions that I want to bring it up here. Even after all my years of trading experience, I'll occasionally suffer a big red day or "drawdown." After a series of red trades—or red days—I realize pretty quickly that what I'm doing is not working. Maybe the market went cold, and I wasn't quick enough to get off the throttle.

Whatever the reason, the first order of business is to stop the bleeding. I'll check myself into what I call "trader rehab" which is not a physical place, but a state of mind where I return to strict guardrails. I have an entire course that discusses trader rehab, but for purposes of this discussion, I do three things:

1. **I set a maximum share size with my broker.** Typically I set my max share size (how many shares I can hold at one time) at about one-half or one-quarter of my regular max share size. For example, if my reduced max size is 10,000, I might have traded 25,000 shares during the day but I cannot be holding more than 10,000 shares in that position at any one time.

2. **I also reduce my maximum daily loss to about one-half or one-quarter of my regular max loss.** Depending on how I'm feeling, I may set that number as a reminder to myself, or I may actually call my broker and ask them to enforce it on their backend. That way, it will happen automatically for me and I don't have to worry about another big red day while I'm in trader rehab.

3. **If I'm in a particularly bad drawdown, I'll take just one trade a day for five days.** My goal is to have five small green days in a row. That means I'll need to be very picky about which trade I'm willing to take each day. If I have a red day, that's okay too, but I have to cut the loss as soon as I realize the trade isn't working.

Even though the first five days of intense trader rehab may only produce a small profit, the purpose isn't about making money. It's about putting space between me and the big loss, and about regaining my confidence. Every time I do a period of trader rehab, I'm impressed by how much better I feel four or five days into it.

I find that if I widen the guardrails too soon, I risk what I call "stair-stepping down" in my trading-account value or equity curve. That means after a period of an ascending equity curve, I have a drawdown, then go sideways for a couple of days before suffering another big loss. This makes my equity curve look like a staircase, and it's going down. This is not okay with me. In order to prevent an extended period of decline, I keep those guardrails firmly in place until I've recouped about half of the drawdown. By that time, my confidence will be back and I'll almost certainly be in a much better place to increase share size and the number of trades I'm taking each day.

The hunt for another Holy Grail

In Chapter 2, I described how I hunted for a Holy Grail in the form of an automated system to find and trade the "perfect" setup or pattern. There's another type of Holy Grail, which involves jumping from one strategy to another, or one technical indicator to another.

Some traders will spend tremendous amounts of time and energy searching for the perfect combination of indicators and strategies in the hope that this combination will always give them winning trades. Of course it makes sense to be on the lookout for profitable strategies, but that's not the motivation of these traders. Just below the surface is a deep fear of loss. It's a desire to search endlessly—and it truly is endless—for that perfect strategy that will prevent them from experiencing any more losses.

You can identify traders with this fear because they'll work to create an automated trading system (as I did, early on), or they will try to mirror-trade someone, or they'll simply jump from one shiny object (strategy) to another. Unfortunately, this quest often continues until their financial resources dry up, and they quit. The way to counteract this behavior is to be aware of it, and then to accept that loss is an inseparable part of day trading.

> "The real Holy Grail is to have self-awareness of stress, and the discipline to follow your rules, regardless of momentary urges."

Kids will join Little League and soon realize that no one in the history of the game of baseball has ever batted 1.000. Strikeouts are simply part of the game. Legendary players still strike out, but they're remembered for their composure under stress, and their ability to execute on their game plan, despite that stress. They are mental role models. The real Holy Grail is to have self-awareness of stress, and the discipline to follow your rules, regardless of momentary urges.

It's time to shift gears from abstract concepts of risk, fear, and discipline, and learn how day traders can get an astonishing amount of information from one glance at a screen. The trick has to do with candlesticks.

CHAPTER 9

Introduction to Candlesticks

WHEN DAY TRADERS SIT DOWN and turn on their computers, they look at several screens of information. One screen shows them the "gappers" or stocks that are set to open the highest relative to where they closed the previous day. Another screen is a real-time feed of news related to selected stocks. More than one screen will be devoted to looking at charts of individual stocks, in the form of "candlesticks."

A stock chart is a visual representation of the price history of a stock. Stock charts provide us with a context so we can quickly understand the current price of a stock relative to previous prices. The most-commonly used charts for day traders are candlestick charts.

Candlestick charts were first used in the 1700s to track the price changes of rice in Japan.[19] They are an efficient way to display a lot of information, especially when you view multiple candlesticks over time. Figure 9-1 shows some basic terminology of candlesticks.

If you are looking at a daily chart that includes the last ninety days, you will see ninety candlesticks. On that chart, each candlestick represents one day of trading. If you're looking at the one-minute chart, then each candlestick is one minute of trading.

Charts can be set in almost any time interval a trader desires, but the most-common ones for candlestick charts are daily, sixty-minute, fifteen-minute, five-minute, and one-minute. I set up my monitors to show daily, five-minute, and one-minute charts. I even have a ten-second chart for when stocks are moving really quickly.

What the candlestick reveals

A single candlestick provides us with four pieces of information about the price action of a stock within a specific interval like daily, fifteen-minute, and so on.

The four pieces of information we learn from the candlestick are:

---

[19] https://en.wikipedia.org/wiki/Candlestick_chart

1. the high of the period;
2. the low of the period;
3. price at the open of the period, and
4. price at the close of the period.

When I say "open" and "close" of the period, I mean the beginning and end prices for that one candlestick, which will be five minutes if it's a five-minute chart, or a full day if it's a daily chart. Investors are accustomed to thinking about the open and close in terms of where a stock began and ended trading for the day. Day traders refer to open and close as it relates to the individual candles on the chart they're viewing.

The thick center of the candlestick or candle is called the "real body" or "body" and the thin lines that go up to the high, and down to the low, are called the upper and lower "candle wicks," "wicks," or "shadows."

On your trading monitor, candles will come in two colors: a green candle means that the opening or initial price for the period was at the bottom of the body, and the close for that interval was at the top of the body. The stock price went up for that interval. The opposite is true for a red candle. In order to show this same information in a black-and-white book, we'll use arrows as seen in Figure 9-1.

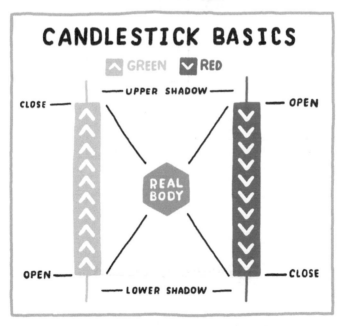

Figure 9-1: Anatomy of a candlestick

Besides the four data points, we can also draw conclusions about market sentiment based on the shape of the candle. Multiple candlesticks lined up together can begin to form familiar chart patterns, with names like "flags," "wedges," and even something called a "dead-cat bounce," as you will learn over time.

With a little practice, you will be able to glance at a set of candlesticks and in a few seconds you'll understand how that stock has been behaving over the different intervals like daily, fifteen-minute, and so on.

Let's look at some of the most-common types of candlesticks that you'll see.

Doji candlesticks

A doji candlestick has a very small candle body, meaning the open price and close price are nearly the same, as you can see in Figure 9-2.

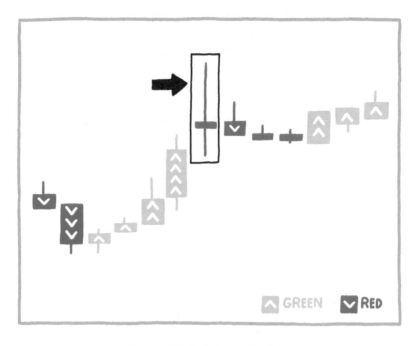

Figure 9-2: A doji candlestick

We can infer from this candlestick shape that there is a momentary standoff between buyers and sellers. If this type of candle happens on heavy volume, it tells us there is a battle at that price.

Sometimes a doji will also have a long upper or lower candle wick. The price suddenly moved up or down, but quickly returned to the same price as the open. This means the move was not sustained.

In general, doji candles represent some indecision in the market. When a doji candle occurs at the top of a very strong move of 5-10 green candles, the indecision reflected in the candle shape can signify a potential reversal. Dojis that happen during a period of sideways consolidation are less important to us, because sideways price action already reflects indecision.

Be patient

If this all feels overwhelming at first, please give yourself time to absorb it. Learning about candlesticks and charts is very much like learning a language. At first, none of it makes sense. Then you learn a few words, and that's progress. The problem is that you then need to understand how individual words fit together into sentences. Soon you're overwhelmed because native speakers are talking at full speed, and you recognize maybe one percent of what they're saying at first. It can be daunting and even depressing.

Then you realize that even little kids can pick up a new language if they're given some time. It's the same with understanding day trading charts. At first it's a lot to recognize doji candles versus many other patterns, never mind how they fit together. But you need to trust me on this: the human brain is *great* at recognizing complex patterns, if given time to see them again and again.

At this stage, simply read through my descriptions, and absorb whatever makes sense. Plan on going through this material again a few times, because each time you'll get a deeper understanding. In Chapter 12 you'll read how Graham, one of my community members, said he had to go through my material *six times* before he was comfortable with it.

Bottoming tails and topping tails

When you see candles with super-long upper or lower wicks, these are called "topping tail" or "bottoming tail" candles. These candles can signify a potential reversal. An example is in Figure 9-3.

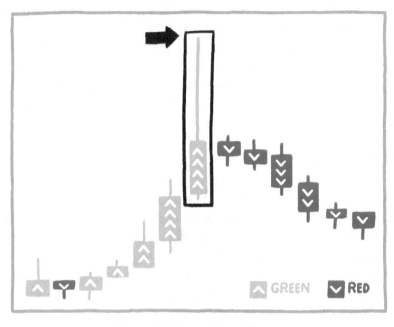

Figure 9-3: A topping tail

To unpack what happened in the candle highlighted in Figure 9-3, the thick body of the candle indicates it started more or less inline with the close of the previous candle, but then shot up. It then closed the period back down not far from where it opened. There had been a continuation of the upward trend, but it was followed by a quick reversal with a close around the middle or low of the candle's range.

This sort of doji candle with long upper or lower wicks is one of my favorite indicators of a potential reversal. I rely on these candlestick patterns to tell me when to exit a winning position or when to back away from buying more shares and wait for a possible reversal.

Hammers and inverted hammers

Like dojis and bottoming tails, the hammer candlestick really only has significance when it happens in the context of a long downtrend. Look at Figure 9-4, where there have been several red or down candlesticks before this hammer candle:

Figure 9-4: Hammer candle (inverted hammers occur after an uptrend)

Hammer candles will always have small bodies and long lower wicks that are larger than the bodies. It is often said that a hammer candle at the bottom of a downtrend is hammering out a new base. The long bottom wick indicates a selloff in that period. Prices dipped down, and then buyers quickly took the opportunity to jump in and push prices back up.

This does not always mean the downward trend will reverse. Confirmation of the reversal will come when the next candle breaks the high of the hammer. This is called a "candle-over-candle" confirmation.

An inverted hammer only carries significance when it occurs at the end of a long uptrend. The inverted hammer has a long topping tail or wick and a small body. The long topping tail indicates a surge of buying that was quickly reversed. This suggests indecision and a battle of sorts between buyers and sellers, that was won by the sellers.

When we're watching stocks trading in real time, we can see the actual formation of these candle wicks. They often appear as a final burst of volume, and then a quick, powerful snap back up as the reversal begins. Again, all of this will make sense over time; just absorb what you can.

Long body candles

The final candlestick shape I'll cover is the long body candle, as you can see in Figure 9-5.

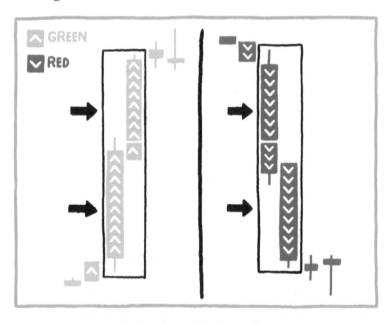

Figure 9-5: Long body candles

As with every other type of candle, it can be green or red. A long body candle that is green opens and surges up without ever going down. These candles close at the high and are an indication of extreme bullish sentiment.

As day traders, we always want to be holding a stock while a long body candle—and the bullish sentiment—is forming. But we must be cautious when considering buying after a long body candle. If we do buy at the top of a long body candle, we're chasing a large move. It's usually better if we wait for a pullback opportunity if we want to trade with the trend. As you learn more about patterns and technical indicators, you will discover how to identify a pullback and many other types of opportunities.

A red long body candle shows the opposite: extreme bearish sentiment as the candle opens and sells off the entire candlestick period. After a series of several long body candles in a row, there is a high likelihood of a bounce or change in sentiment.

———◼◼◼———

Individual candlesticks come in a great variety of shapes, with different meanings. Then when you consider several candles in a row, you get much more information. You can receive yet more insights when you learn how to look at the candlestick charts for a single stock over several intervals. As I mentioned at the beginning of this chapter, I always have open the charts that show daily, five-minute, one-minute, and ten-second movements.

Candlestick shapes and patterns are just the beginning of technical analysis. To fully interpret price action we must look at volume, which is the number of shares traded. High and low volume during a candlestick period provide deeper insight into the shape of the candlestick and the level of interest among traders.

To further interpret candlestick charts and price action, many traders will rely on popular technical indicators such as moving averages, the Volume Weighted Average Price, Moving Average Convergence Divergence, and the Relative Strength Index, among others. These are beyond the scope of this book, but not difficult to understand. Most technical indicators are lagging indicators, meaning they require price changes before they create signals. Looking directly at candlesticks forming on your charts will provide the most real-time view of the stock.

The human brain is astonishingly good at pattern recognition. Just think about all the different faces you instantly recognize, and how you also can interpret facial expressions from moment to moment. Once you apply that powerful brain of yours to the pattern recognition of candlestick charts, you'll soon be seeing stock movements in a whole new way.

So far in this book we have talked a great deal about what it takes to be a good day trader, in terms of knowledge, skills, emotional awareness, and discipline. You may also wonder what it takes for a stock to be a good candidate for day trading. That's what we'll discuss in the next chapter.

CHAPTER 10

Finding the Right Stocks to Trade

AS I HOPE YOU'VE GATHERED BY NOW, by far the biggest determinants of your day trading success are elements in your head: your knowledge, discipline, attitude, and ability to control your emotions. It's no accident that I have used the first chapters in this book to cover those key topics.

It's time to bring in some other concepts. Even if you've never day traded, you may know day traders look for particular stock-trading patterns. We focus on the candlestick charts of various durations until we see something we think could be worth taking a position in.

It would be a mistake to think that day trading is all about the pattern, even though if you watch me trade, the candlestick charts and ever-changing patterns are the most-visible aspects of the trade.

The question of which pattern to use is beyond this book. There are a great many patterns and you'll have plenty of time to test and select which ones you like the most when you're using the trading simulator. I have a few favorites, which you'll certainly get to know if you keep watching me on YouTube or become a member over at Warrior Trading.

Patterns are indeed important, but the pattern itself is not a day trading strategy—it's just a pattern. Similar patterns occur with other financial instruments like commodities and cryptocurrency. A day trading strategy involves much more than the pattern, and includes the following:

- **Maximum acceptable loss.** We already discussed this in Chapter 7, both in terms of loss per trade, and overall loss for the day.

- **Daily profit goals.** As we discussed in Chapter 7, you need to know both your target profit by trade, and your overall daily number.

- **Share price.** I focus on stocks priced between $2 and $20. Occasionally I'll trade something outside these parameters, but it's important to have a focus.

- **Time of day.** I already discussed in Chapter 3 how the vast majority of trading happens between 7:30 am and 11:30 am Eastern.

- **Which stock to focus on.** This is the element that we'll now cover, starting with the next guardrail:

— GUARDRAIL #12 —

I've found that trading the right stock is much more important than trading the right pattern.

To put it another way, if you trade the wrong stock—even with a great pattern that's made you money in the past—you will find the stock is unpredictable, you'll be super frustrated, and you will more than likely lose money.

So what makes a stock strong? Let's go through the six components to the answer.

Strong Stock Component #1: A stock that's volatile *right now*. You have already heard that as day traders, we should be hunters of volatility and managers of risk. We've covered many risk-reduction strategies already. Now let's focus on the volatility.

We discussed in Chapter 8 how risk and fear are always present when we trade; it's also pretty obvious that greed is a potent motivator, especially with untrained and undisciplined traders. These are the people who are guided by gut feelings instead of a trading plan that involves profit/loss ratios, target profits, and maximum acceptable losses. No matter how high a stock has gone, they can make a case for it to go much higher.

What turns these emotions into a volatile stock is some sort of catalyst, usually in the form of news. It might be an announcement that the Food and Drug Administration has cleared a drug or device to be sold, or the release of an un-expectedly strong earnings report. If it's big enough news, it will drive a move in the stock.

> "There's a certain conventional wisdom about investing that says we should "buy low and sell high." That's not a momentum day trading strategy. Instead, we buy high and sell higher."

As I said before, I'm not interested in stocks that might move, are "primed" to move, or are "significantly undervalued." I only focus on stocks that *are already* moving. That typically means that they're up by 15 to 20 percent or more since yesterday.

There's a certain conventional wisdom about investing that says we should "buy low and sell high." That's not a momentum day trading strategy. Instead, we buy high and sell higher. The benefit of buying high is that the stock is already moving substantially, which spares me the uncertainty about which stocks might move.

Once I buy, if the stock continues to go up, I'll sell higher, then if it forms a new pattern, I may buy it again with a somewhat smaller position, and hope to sell even higher. Scaling down share size as a stock moves higher is a way of reducing risk while continuing to capitalize on the momentum.

Another bit of conventional wisdom says that avoiding losses is a good thing. Although I agree with that statement in general, I use loss to my advantage: I will keep buying and selling higher until I reach my first loss, where the stock did not go higher.

Why would I do that? Because it means I was able to ride that stock as far as possible, while carefully adjusting my risk exposure.

The best opportunities in the market are the ones that are the most volatile, with the highest relative volume. We'll discuss more about relative volume later in this chapter, but that combination of volatility and volume leads us to the next guardrail:

GUARDRAIL #13

Each day when I sit down and am looking at potential stocks to trade, I ask myself: *Is this the strongest stock today?*

You may have learned in school that the first person to cross the Atlantic Ocean non-stop by airplane was Charles Lindbergh. Who was the second person? No one is taught that. (It was Amelia Earhart.[20]) It's the same with stocks on the move: today's strongest, most volatile stock gets flashed across the screens of traders worldwide. It's at the top of the list, by definition in the #1 slot. It gets the most attention, and that gives us the volatility and relative volume that we seek.

Keep in mind that occasionally the #1 top gainer is not the most obvious stock to trade. Sometimes it will be too expensive (over $20) or too cheap (under $1). Other times the #1 top gainer will be a stock that has just been acquired. When a stock is a buyout, the value becomes fixed at the buyout price and volatility disappears. When a stock is a leading gainer but not the most obvious stock for retail traders, then the second or third leader may end up taking the spotlight.

Besides knowing which is the strongest stock today, you should be mindful of whether the overall market is hot or cold. On some days it seems like you could throw a dart at the stock listings in a newspaper and be likely to hit a stock on the move. Then there are days where very little seems to move, and where even the best-moving stock is anemic. In periods of market lethargy, scale back your expectations for making great trades, or even for making any trades.

Strong Stock Component #2: Fear in the market. Disciplined day traders usually see fear in the market as an opportunity. Remember from our earlier discussion that stocks don't move by themselves, or even based on news. They move when traders react.

FOMO, or Fear Of Missing Out, is a huge driver of stock volatility. Traders watch that strongest stock of the day and may see

---

[20] https://www.si.edu/object/lockheed-vega-5b-amelia-earhart%3Anasm_
A19670093000#:~:text=Amelia%20Earhart%20is%20probably%20the,solo%20across%20
the%20Atlantic%20Ocean.

> "Fear of loss is a powerful motivator for traders. It makes people capitulate and buy stocks way too high, and it also makes some people panic and bail out of positions."

that it ripped up 50 percent in mere minutes. They know that someone just sold that stock for a nice profit, and then they see the stock go even higher. It's a breeding ground for irrational trading.

It's even happened to me. Someone in my chat room will tell me they've made $50 grand on today's big mover. I pretty much cannot help but feel FOMO over that! But I can control whether *I give in to FOMO*. If I emotionally smash the buy button thinking only about potential profit, it is a form of emotional hijack.

On the other hand, if the stock is forming another one of my favorite chart patterns, we could see a continued move higher. This can be an opportunity to capitalize on FOMO in the market that's driving the stock higher, without falling victim to FOMO myself. It's like walking a tightrope: you can quickly fall if you get unbalanced by adding to your position too high or by getting stubborn about bailing out of a losing position.

Fear of loss is a powerful motivator for traders. It makes people capitulate and buy stocks way too high, and it also makes some people panic and bail out of positions. They may feel that they've bought too high and they now throw in the towel out of fear or anger. FOMO fuels volatility.

The approach that works the best for me is to keep trading as a stock is going up, but if I give back approximately 10-15 percent of my profit on the day, I shut it down before I give back more. If I find myself in a position where it appears that I bought too high, I ruthlessly cut my loss. This is the mark of a disciplined trader.

Strong Stock Component #3: Greed in the market. You can think of greed in the market as one-day-old FOMO. It's common for one stock or another to make eye-popping moves within a single day. A hot stock in a strong market can move by hundreds of percent in a day. Not only does that stock make it to the top of the leaderboard for the day, but the effect can continue after the close. Some traders think: *I can't believe that I didn't get any of that runup. I was right there,* *watching the whole thing happen before my eyes! Just half of that gain would have made my month...*

When this happens, there will be some traders who missed that move and who will try to make up for it tomorrow. That fear and greed is so strong that it spills over to the next trading session.

Politicians refer to a "coat-tail effect" where one strong candidate sometimes has the effect of sweeping other candidates along, too. I see that same thing happen in the market. Sometimes when one stock is strong, I'll see three or four others start to pick up. I call it sympathy momentum. It's not that the fundamentals of those other stocks suddenly changed; it's the emotional momentum of traders looking for the next big move. In analyzing my trade history, I've noticed that typically my biggest winners are all very close together; unfortunately, so have been my biggest losers.

> **"...each day we have a reservoir of willpower, and the tank was reading zero when we went for that last trade."**

The power of ten to fifteen cents

I speak with many successful traders, and I've noticed a phenomenon that's happened to me, too. They'll tell me how they had a good day trading, and decided they were done for the day. Then a half hour or so later, they went in for one last trade—and lost all their profit for the day.

This happens because each day we have a reservoir of willpower, and the tank was reading zero when we went for that last trade. It's fine and even necessary to trade as aggressively as you can, but it's even more important to pull some of your profit out of the market and know when to quit. That brings us to the next guardrail:

— GUARDRAIL #14 —

My goal each day is to pull ten to fifteen cents per share out of the market.

You may be scratching your head at that one. It doesn't sound like much of a goal, right? Believe me—it separates the professional, consistent, successful traders from all the rest.

If you can do just ten cents per share per day consistently, that's something you can scale. When you're trading 100 shares, that $10 profit doesn't seem like much of an achievement. But at 1,000 shares, we're talking $100 per day and with 5,000 shares, it's $500 per day.

As simple as it sounds to pull out a dime a day, that's a solid first goal. It will require being disciplined about trading the right stocks and taking really good quality entries, where you decide your risk/reward ratio looks good and you pull the trigger on the trade.

"You can join that elite group if you show that you consistently pull a dime per share out of the market."

This concept is vital to your success as a trader, because it helps to keep you from swinging for home runs too soon. When you first learn to trade, it's natural to want to validate that day trading is worth all the effort. The best validation would be to make a bunch of money, but the problem is that your account is not large. It's therefore natural to want to swing for the fences and get that home run.

If I was looking at your trading history, I would not be impressed by the occasional home run; that might be due to chance. I'd be impressed by your long string of ten-cent base hits.

Just so you know, this advice is harder to follow than it seems, and I'm still subject to it in my own trading. I recently took a position on a stock at around $9.80 and it ripped right up to $10.50. I was up seventy cents a share! I didn't take any of it off the table. (In other words, I didn't sell a portion of my position and keep the rest, in order that I might profit from a further increase.) This was an awesome trade, and I held the entire position. It ended up coming back to break-even. That was not a smart move. I should have scaled out as the stock went up.

Just so you have some perspective, most seasoned traders do not take a full dollar per share out of the market per day. For most, it's probably anywhere from 15 to 25 cents. On a good day it will be 50 cents and on an amazing day it will be a dollar or more. Remember that I'm talking about the survivors here—the people who have dedicated

> "The goal is to identify these daily unicorns and to be disciplined about how you will trade them. If you can do those two things regularly, you just might succeed in this profession."

their time and energy to learning this profession and who are disciplined. You can join that elite group if you show that you consistently pull a dime per share out of the market.

Strong Stock Component #4: An imbalance between supply and demand. Each morning we are looking for stocks that have the potential to move 20 or 30 percent at a minimum. On a really strong day we might see 300 percent or 400 percent moves. What creates such situations? It's when there is an incredible demand for a stock against a very limited supply.

This concept comes back to the float, which is the number of shares that have been sold on the market and are available to trade. But remember that for any stock, you have some shareholders that are not interested in selling their shares. The actual number of shares truly available to trade on any day is even lower.

Let's look at a situation that I see as I'm writing this: it's a stock with the symbol of OBLN. I can see on my screen that it has a float of 6 million shares, and it traded 321 million shares today. On this day, OBLN is the darling: it's the most-traded and most-visible stock.

Just think about those numbers: how many times have traders bought and sold 6 million shares so that the total has reached 321 million shares? That should give you a sense of the intense focus that the most-visible stock gets on any given day in the market. The goal is to identify these daily unicorns and to be disciplined about how you will trade them. If you can do those two things regularly, you just might succeed in this profession.

Strong Stock Component #5: High relative volume. The relative volume metric is where you will see amazing differences between the most volatile stocks and all the rest.

It is not unheard of for the most volatile stock to trade 1,500 shares on one day, and 300 million shares on the next. This does not happen every day, but when it does, it's usually after some catalyst, like news about the company. Then instantly some algorithmic trading systems will execute orders literally before any humans can react.

Next thing we know, retail traders jump in. The stock now is at the top of the list of active stocks worldwide, and things continue from there. Some traders sell into this strength, having taken their initial profits. Others will see the excitement and will hesitate, then buy out of FOMO.

You will commonly see three numbers relating to a stock's volume:

1. The float, which is how many shares are available to trade;
2. Total volume today; and
3. Relative volume.

That last number is expressed as a multiple of average volume. For example, if the average volume is 150,000 shares per day and yesterday it traded 300,000 shares, the relative volume will be 2.0. The higher the relative volume, the better. That's because it indicates a sudden interest in the stock, which typically results from some catalyst. In addition, the technical patterns that we use to trade generally respond better when the trading volumes are above average.

Strong Stock Component #6: Former runner status. We've already discussed at some length how FOMO can have powerful effects on stocks.

> "It's important to recognize stocks that are a distraction from what is truly the most obvious stock."

My point now is that once a stock has been the focus of that mentality, it establishes something of a reputation. It's gotten exposure on countless trading screens and chat rooms and that exposure lingers, not only for the next few trading days, but in the minds of traders.

Any time that stock starts to pop up, it seems to get extra attention. If there is a strong daily chart or fresh news, traders are quick to jump in. They remember how strong this stock was in a previous trading session.

I have a scanner that specifically filters stocks I consider former runners. I set the total volume filters lower on that stock, because when a former runner starts to move, I want to make sure I see it quickly.

During hot cycles, we see a combination of former runners, fresh top gainers, and multi-day momentum stocks that keep trending higher.

I generally find that it's better to trade with the pack, in the sense of focusing on the stock with the highest volume. Sometimes a former runner becomes the most obvious stock of the day, but other times they become a bit of a distraction. It's important to recognize stocks that are a distraction from what is truly the most obvious stock.

This is a skill that you will gain over time. However, one of the metrics I look at to tell the difference is relative volume: if it isn't high—former runner or not—that stock probably is not the right trade for today.

Another guardrail is in order here:

GUARDRAIL #15

I look not only for the strongest stock today, but I also ask myself: *Is this the obvious one?*

If you had to talk yourself into trading the stock, it won't be any more obvious to all the other traders, and it's not worth trading. Better to wait for something else to happen during this trading session, or wait for a new day.

———■———

You can be forgiven if your head is swimming with day trading concepts, given how many we've covered so far. I'm not done, because in the next chapter you will find out about several more guardrails that have helped to reduce my day trading risk.

CHAPTER 11

Getting Better and Better

IN THE PREVIOUS CHAPTERS, I've covered fifteen guardrails that I had to learn the hard way. These guardrails, when implemented properly, can help reduce unnecessary losses as a day trader. To give you every advantage I wish I'd had when I got started, here are five more guardrails.

GUARDRAIL #16

In retrospect, my goal should have been that I would be ready to trade when I had proven that I was ready; not when I merely thought it was time.

Despite all my warnings about how hard day trading is, you might have become enthusiastic about the profession by this point. I think you can tell that I find day trading to be rewarding on many levels. On top of that, here you are, having read this far into my book. I can't blame you if you want to put the book down already, open a brokerage account, and get going with placing that first trade.

Don't do it. *Successful* day trading requires a high level of knowledge and discipline. As smart as I'm sure you are, and as good as I think this book is, you don't yet have all the elements in place to become a profitable day trader. Later in this chapter I'll describe the very next steps you might take in order to continue building a solid foundation for beginning your day trading career. But right now I want to remind you about the phenomenal tool you can use to save yourself all kinds of grief and money.

I'm talking about trading simulators.

I discussed the simulator or "sim" in Chapters 3 and 5, but I want to emphasize it again. So much in business and life is comprised of gray areas and judgment calls. Not with the sim: for any period, you're either red or green. (Yes, you could be exactly even but that is rare.)

Even though you can close this book right now and start trading in a sim, I suggest you not do that. On the one hand, I'm a believer in beginner's luck and you might just have it; but you may also find that you lose so much money, so quickly, that you give up on the whole idea of day trading.

What you should instead consider doing is finish your first stages of learning—from this book and from the next steps I'll describe shortly—and then ease yourself into the sim. It's much better than to be thrown into the deep end when you're not trained for it.

Let me give you a preview of what you're likely to discover as you begin to trade, as seen in Figure 11-1:

Figure 11-1: The stages many day traders go through

Of course, this is not some statistical finding, but is my impression, after having dealt with a great many traders over the years. Let's look more closely at each phase, and the associated emotions.

- **Beginner's luck.** *Day trading is EASY! I just sat here, clicked a few buttons, and made cold hard cash!*
- **Overconfidence.** *Sims are for losers. I seem to be a natural at this.*
- **Frustration.** *What's happening? It was going so well, and suddenly I've given it all back and then some!* (Many people quit here.)

- **No visible progress.** *I can't believe how hard day trading is! I'm sticking with it, but it's two steps forward and three steps back!* (More people quit here.)
- **The slow climb.** *I've been at this for a long time, and I'm just breakeven?* (Still more quit here.)

As I described in my own journey in Chapter 2, it took me a while to realize that breakeven is an accomplishment. Only after I identified my winning strategies and stopped the losing strategies, did I begin to see consistent progress.

What I did not know at the time—but you do now—is that you don't have to experience all these phases with real money on the line. The sim is your friend, where you can experiment, learn, and hone your skills until you're producing regular green weeks. I know of no better way to learn this profession.

Later in this chapter I will give you more details on when you're ready to transition from the sim to trading with real money.

— GUARDRAIL #17 —

I keep a trading journal, and update it after each trading day.

Earlier I told you it was only when I studied my past trades—when I was broke and down to my last shot at trading—that I found a way out. A path to climbing back to profitability. That insight did not come to me in a dream: it resulted from hard work to uncover patterns I hadn't noticed before then.

In the heat of trading it's tough enough to keep a clear head, beat back your emotions, and stay within the guardrails as you trade. That's asking a lot. But if you take the time after trading hours to study your trades, pretty soon you'll gain insights.

Some good tools exist that take some of the manual labor out of the process, but it's also possible to keep your journal right on a simple spreadsheet. You should track the type of setup, time, symbol, entry price, exit price, amount made or lost, and notes.

I don't mean to suggest that you should stop every few moments to log this information into your journal; there may not be time for

"Bringing both positive and negative habits of your trading into your awareness is an important step in refining and improving a strategy."

that in the heat of trading. Instead, all the information is available to grab after your trading session. Just don't put it off for days hoping you can catch up on it over the weekend. It needs to become a quick habit, while the trades are fresh in your mind and while the "notes" section will describe what you were thinking at the time.

Though you capture your journal data daily, you might review it daily or every few days, depending on how successful you've been lately. You're looking to get a deeper understanding of where you have strengths and successes, and where you need to make adjustments. For example, you might notice that most of your profits happen in the morning and your biggest losses are in the afternoon. Now you can make a note to review the guardrails before afternoon trading and be more mindful of that pattern. Bringing both positive and negative habits of your trading into your awareness is an important step in refining and improving a strategy.

This brings us to the next guardrail:

GUARDRAIL #18

I regularly analyze my journal for clues about the conditions that generate green and red days for me. When I'm in a slump, I study my journal even more.

Even what appears to be trivial improvements can really add up over time. If you trade 50,000 shares per month and you can improve your average profits by one single cent per share, it will increase your profits by $500 per month.

Another way to look at it is the difference between success and failure in this business can be a matter of only a slight adjustment in your ratios. When you're reviewing your trades, first notice where you may have violated one or more guardrails. That's no-brainer analysis, because it's not like you need to scrutinize the statistics in order to discover a hidden insight. Maybe in the heat of trading, you ignored your max loss. For the next trading session, you'll have something specific to write yourself a note about and watch out for.

The day trading personality

I've met a lot of great people in the day trading community. They're from many walks of life: rich and poor; highly educated and dropout; men and women; from many countries…the list goes on.

There seems at least one common personality trait among the sort of people who are attracted to day trading: they are independent thinkers. We live in a culture that values concepts like "slow and steady wins the race," but we day traders want to win that race NOW. We're looking to make a month's worth of conventional investing profits in a day. We're willing to endure the awkward silences and uncomfortable reactions that follow when we tell people we're day traders.

The very independence that gives us the strength to be in this business can also work against us at times. I'll give you a couple of examples.

On several occasions I've spoken with traders who've gone through my training and are having problems. When I ask for details about exactly what they're doing, I come to find out that they are day trading using a mobile app on their phone. That is a mistake. I am aware of NO professional day traders who base their business on a trading app on their cell phone. In order to succeed at this difficult profession, you need to have several windows open on your laptop or desktop, and you need to be fully present and not multitasking on your phone. Of course many people already know my opinion on trying to use apps instead of a computer, but some try it anyway. I would say this is a trader being "independent" by ignoring the experience it's taken me over a decade to accumulate.

Another example is when I'm discussing strategies with someone and he says: "Oh, I can't do what you're suggesting because I'm trading with a $700 account." I think it's great when people start out—after trading in the sim—with a small trading account, and build it up from there.

The problem happens when this person has a bit of success, builds it up from $500 to say $2,700, and decides to pull $2,000 out of that account to spend on other stuff. Yes, it's their money and they can do whatever they want with it. But the reality is that you have more options and flexibility when your account is larger. Day trading is at its hardest and slowest when your account is tiny, with only $500 or so to trade with. So why are you making it perpetually challenging on yourself by pulling out all of your profits and starting back at the minimum?

> "Day trading is at its hardest and slowest when your account is tiny, with only $500 or so to trade with. So why are you making it perpetually challenging on yourself by pulling out all of your profits and starting back at the minimum?"

I created a video in which I talk about my hobby of maple sugaring and how that relates to day trading.[21] In case you don't know, maple sugaring involves collecting the sap from sugar maple trees in the late winter, and boiling it down into maple syrup. There is a traditional way to do it, and then there's the way that professionals now do it, given how technology has advanced. Whether it's maple sugaring or day trading, you need to look at how the successful professionals approach the business, instead of deciding that you know better and want to do it differently.

— GUARDRAIL #19 —

In retrospect, I've realized that I could have saved a lot of effort and money by resisting the temptation to blaze a new trail. When I'm learning something new, I now follow what the professionals do as much as I possibly can.

You are an independent-thinking beginner. Successful day traders are independent-thinking professionals, and yet the vast majority of

---

[21] https://youtu.be/X8tpTL4povQ

them follow certain common practices. You are undertaking a challenging profession. It's a mistake to decide to blaze a new trail with your ideas about how to take a shortcut to success, or cherry pick the concepts you wish to follow. The only real shortcut to success is to not make the mistakes that other people made who came before you. Stand on their shoulders and follow proven principles. If and when you become successful, by all means innovate away.

What now?

If I've done my job in this book, you should be thinking one of two thoughts at this point:

1. *Wow, I'm pretty sure that day trading is not for me! I thought it might be a cool little hobby that I could do now and then. Easy money. It sounds like a lot of work to get good at it.*

2. *I didn't know what day trading was really about, but I have a better sense now. I feel like I may have the personality and interest to pull this off. What I don't know are the exact next steps I need to take, in order to continue to learn about day trading.*

If #1 sounds more like you, then reading this book has been time well spent! You've saved yourself all kinds of difficulty and cost to find out that day trading is not a good fit. Who knows: maybe your circumstances might change and day trading will turn into a good option for you to pursue down the road.

If #2 sounds more like you, then I'm glad that you've found this book to be useful. Fortunately, the next steps in your journey are pretty clear.

Before we get into it, a warning: **do not become discouraged by the amount you need to learn!** You're not in a race and besides, you probably have lots of skills, sports, hobbies, and other activities that are made up of many dozens of individual micro-skills. I know I'm a broken record here, but I also know how beginners need encouragement to keep on going. From time to time, all of us need it.

Step 1: Build a solid basic foundation of day trading knowledge.

In this book I've been able to cram in merely an overview of the concepts you need to know in order to even sit down at a sim and begin to trade. As safe as a sim is, it's a mistake to not build your knowledge base before trading there. That's because you can easily become discouraged and throw in the towel if you don't have that knowledge in place.

The knowledge I'm talking about is not boring, dry textbook stuff. If you've read this far, then I'm pretty sure you'll find it interesting. Here's a list of the next topics you should learn:

Screen deep dive. For each of the windows or screens that you'll have open on your monitor, you must know what all the terms, numbers, chart lines, and patterns mean.

Technical indicators. There are thousands of them, but most are overrated and unnecessary. A technical indicator is a ratio or other metric that may or may not put the current price of a stock in context, so the trader can decide whether to buy, hold, or sell. Study these more-useful ones:

- Simple and Exponential Moving Averages
- Volume Weighted Average Price
- Moving Average Convergence Divergence
- Relative Strength Index

Concepts of support and resistance, and how to determine where past and current ones are for a stock.

Gaps, windows, and triggers are formations you will see in charts, and they can give you insights into what actions you might take.

Types of brokers, and how to decide which one is the best for you to open your first account with.

Order types. When you should use limit orders, market orders, and stop orders. How to execute orders pre-market and after hours, and how to harness the power of advanced order-routing technology.

Level 2. We touched on this, but you must get comfortable with this firehose of useful, real-time data and what it's telling you.

Time and sales. This is another window that shows you each transaction that was executed for a particular stock. This goes hand-in-hand with Level 2.

How to use the order-entry window and hot keys to save time when you're in the thick of trading.

Chart patterns. You can go crazy trying to learn too many patterns, because there is no end to them. At first, get familiar with some of the most-useful ones, at least in my opinion:

- Buying the first and second pullbacks
- Flat-top breakouts

- Flat-bottom breakouts
- Bull flags
- Bear flags
- Moving average retracements
- Buying a higher high after a pullback using a five-minute uptrend
- Parabolic moves
- Head and shoulders
- ABCD patterns

How to use stock-scanning software and build watch lists. Learn how to customize the software so you can sit down in the morning and already have a tight focus on what you might trade that day.

Step 2: Find a strategy that is a good fit for you.

Once you're familiar with the material I listed in Step 1, including the trading patterns, you'll be able to pick a strategy that most resonates with you. Something will stand out.

Just don't try to reinvent the wheel with your own custom strategy at this point; instead, decide on a strategy that someone else has proven to be profitable and learn it. You are not taking any type of "final vows" here, and you can always switch strategies later. Your goal is first to learn one strategy thoroughly, instead of being superficially familiar with a bunch of them.

Step 3: Create or adopt a trading plan based on your strategy.

Your trading plan will be a thorough document that spells out in specific detail how you intend to trade. Here are a few of the items it covers:

- Maximum risk per trade
- Profit target per trade
- Daily profit target
- Trading plan goal
- Number of trades per day
- What price stocks I will trade
- What float will I focus on
- What time of day I will trade
- When will I stop trading

And many more. It's specific enough that you could hand it to another trader and they'd have a very clear idea of what to do, when. It's similar to a pilot's flight plan, which is a detailed description of the destination, route across the country, different altitudes, and so on. Trading plans and flight plans still leave room for judgment, but they are how professionals plan their actions.

I provide members at Warrior Trading with "Ross's Day Trading Plan for Beginners." It's the plan I've used every time I've done a small account challenge. My trading plan is based on a momentum strategy and includes a position-management technique designed to capture small "base hit" winners with high accuracy.

The drawback to higher accuracy is a lower profit-to-loss ratio. I'm okay with this because as a beginner trader, high accuracy is important for boosting confidence. Whether you use my trading plan or one from another trader, what's important is for you to have the discipline to follow it, and that you carefully review your metrics as you accumulate historical data.

Step 4: Trade in a sim.

I will modify this advice just a little to say that if you open a small account and use real money—but tiny position sizes—that could work, too. Some traders prefer this over sim trading, in order to begin the process of emotionally conditioning themselves to experiencing loss. My main problem is that it can become a slippery slope. A trader may not intend to trade with anything

> "Every beginner makes plenty of mistakes; because they are inevitable, it's better that those mistakes have as little financial effect as possible."

over ten shares, but then enters 1,000 by accident, or becomes emotionally hijacked and starts revenge trading. Whether you use a sim or trade with real money with tiny position sizes, it's important that you feel no monetary pain until you're well along the learning curve. Every beginner makes plenty of mistakes; because they are inevitable, it's better that those mistakes have as little financial effect as possible.

Step 5: Review your metrics regularly in order to make improvements to your strategy.

While still in the sim, continue to lay a strong foundation by focusing on your metrics. The ones you should look at most closely are your accuracy and profit/loss ratio. In addition, monitor the number of weeks in a row that you've been green. We all have red days, so don't sweat that. The real test is to be green for a string of weeks. If you can do that for five or six weeks, something must be working in your profit/loss ratio and accuracy.

Those two measures alone are not enough, because you could have great accuracy and a pretty good profit/loss ratio; but as you read earlier in this book, you still could have one or two big losses that put you in the red overall. That's why it's so important to see the consistency of green weeks before you think about widening those guardrails.

Speaking of guardrails, here's the last one:

— GUARDRAIL #20 —

When starting out, I should have made just one trade per day until I could show five or six green weeks in a row.

That may seem overly restrictive, but it's smart advice. When your goal is a single trade per day, you become very picky about what you're willing to trade. You sit back and watch what's happening and don't jump at the first interesting pattern. Especially when you're starting out and day trading is a firehose of data streaming at you in real time, your #1 goal is to make sense of it, and your #2 goal is to make a trade. So watch intently, study the patterns and data, and make that one trade be the best you can do today. It's the shortest route to building confidence.

By the way, it's a good idea to print out the candlestick charts of stocks that in hindsight were great examples of the strategy you're going for. You are a hunter of volatility and a manager of risk: take a picture of your prey and stick it where you'll see it. You'll be more likely to recognize it quickly, the next time it shows itself.

"But Ross, earlier you said it was a good idea to scale out of a position and not sell your entire position all at once. Now you're saying I should limit myself to one trade at first. How can I scale out with one trade?"

You're right, I did say that! I was referring to the circumstances you will eventually experience, where you have a sizable position and also are making several trades per day. When you're just starting out with one trade of 100 or so shares, it's not practical or necessary to scale out. In this phase, beginner traders take one entry, and hold until they see one of the exit indicators outlined in their trading plan. Once they see that exit indicator, they sell the whole position.

There's one other thing that needs to happen while you're trading in the sim: you need to get through your first drawdown. Even if you're making just one careful trade per day, you will inevitably catch a big loss at some point. Maybe it was an emotional mistake, or maybe the stock just acted crazy and it wasn't something you could have avoided.

It happens, and it needs to happen to you, so you can learn to handle it. You do that not by beating yourself up, but instead by going to your journal and figuring out what was the cause. Remind yourself that you've made many positive trades, and you're still that trader. Then either fix your approach (if you forgot something) or move on and work to recover the sim money you've lost. Once you've made that first recovery from a drawdown, you're ready for a big milestone.

Step 6: After you have those green weeks and have recovered from a drawdown, now begin trading with real money.

The first time you trade with real money, you'll already have some experience and a track record of green weeks. Even so, no matter how good you were in the simulator, you'll discover that trading with real money is different. Therefore, expect an adjustment phase.

How is it different? For one thing, you knew all along that you were trading in a sim. Now, the emotions of trading with real money will change the experience. You'll have the positive boost that comes with thinking to yourself: *I just made more in the last ten minutes than I made in a week at my first job!* Enjoy the moment, but don't let it go to your head, because soon enough you'll be thinking the opposite: *What just happened? How could I have lost that much money in the space of ten minutes?!*

By the way, remember to be careful whom you tell about your real-money trading outcomes. Outsiders who don't know the methodical process you're following may give you the opposite of the support you need: "Are you outta your mind? That's a month's rent you just blew with your little day trading thing." You're better off staying quiet, or giving general descriptions of how things are going.

When you transition to real money, don't be surprised if you feel you've lost a bit of the momentum and confidence you built while in the sim. It's natural, and you know what to do: keep the guardrails in view, execute on your trading plan, and review your journal. You do that, and soon enough you'll build back that momentum and confidence.

Step 7: As your metrics support it, begin scaling up.

This means adjusting the guardrails a *little*. For example, if you've been trading with 100 shares, then move to 200 shares. It will potentially double your profits (and losses) but it will not double the workload the way moving to two trades per day would be. Also, when you increase the number of trades, you're statistically more likely to see one or more red trades, and that risks an emotional setback.

After two or three weeks with your increased share size—assuming you're still pretty consistently green—you can bump the size up again to 300 shares. The goal is slow, incremental increases while trading at the edge of your comfort zone, because you want to grow but not so fast that you risk wrecking your confidence. Acclimate yourself so that you experience those losses and rebuild back. Narrow the guardrails if need be, but focus on bouncing back after the next drawdown.

> **It's far more important to build confidence and skill than it is to build your profits. Do the first two right, and the third will come over time.**

Continue this process until you're making one trade of 1,000 or even 2,000 shares. When you've built your skills and confidence to do that with consistent profits, now's the time to think about scaling up to two trades per day. Then you lather, rinse, and repeat in the sense of building up share size, trying different setups, and so forth. It's far more important to build confidence and skill than it is to build your profits. Do the first two right, and the third will come over time. Profits are a byproduct of a disciplined trader with some experience and educated intuition following a proven trading plan.

The following isn't so much a guardrail as it is a best practice: try to participate in a community of traders where you can surround yourself with like-minded people who are trading in a similar way to you. If you build a trading plan that focuses on trading small caps with a gap-and-go pattern, then ideally you have a few friends in a chat room where you can talk over what you're seeing today. You will benefit four ways from doing this:

1. You will enjoy a camaraderie with fellow traders who "get you" and understand the ups and downs of day trading better than anyone.
2. More eyes on the market at the same time will help to prevent missed opportunities.
3. Over time, you'll develop trust with a few people who can give you honest feedback about what you're doing well, and not so well.
4. You can benefit from mentorship and support from more experienced traders.

In a profession with as much uncertainty as day trading, I can say this for certain: good communities exist where you can get valuable and even crucial support. And you'll make friends, too.

I have something good in store for you in the next two chapters. They are interviews I did with a couple of traders in my community. I think you'll see that they put their own personal stamp on how they trade, while still being solid examples of trading with discipline.

CHAPTER 12

Interview with Graham

Ross: Graham[22] is a member of our community and a momentum trader for sure. Graham, you are trading basically the same strategy that I trade. Pretty much every day, we're looking at the same stocks and everything else. Why don't we get this started with you giving us a little introduction of where you're from, how long you've been trading, and your strategy?

Graham: I'm from New York, and I've been trading for a long time. When I opened my first brokerage account I was dabbling: just buying a stock, selling a stock, and not really knowing what I was doing. Then for a while, I was just trading sideways.[23] I began to trade actively almost every day, but still was just going sideways.

I did that for a couple of years until I joined Warrior Trading. I obviously learned from you, but it wasn't instant for me. It took me a while. I went through your classes probably six times! I was hearing you while I was sleeping, while I was traveling, and in lots of places.

It took some time for me to get a hang of it, because I'm a hard learner. It takes me a while to learn something. But I had a drive to learn it, because I saw people that were making money trading. I could see that it was possible to be profitable doing this, and that's what helped to carry me until I could become a profitable trader.

Ross: Some people will struggle with momentum trading on small caps, because it's like the Wild West sometimes. It can be so fast, like zero to 100 miles an hour, and then back to zero. Some people decide to switch over to large caps, which usually are a little calmer. Not the crazy stuff, but sometimes crazy. Have you ever tried that?

---

[22] Note: I have changed the name of this person in order to respect his privacy. Graham's trading results should not be considered typical, or an indication of a result you should expect.

[23] In other words, being up and down, and not making any progress.

Graham: I did. I branched out, but it was quick. I looked at large caps, but I just didn't see how they would work for me. I didn't see those huge 500 percent, 1,000 percent, or even higher moves. Large caps didn't fit my personality, so that's what brought me back to small-cap stocks.

Ross: Many people know that when I got in trading, I had almost no income. I was spending more money than I was making, so for me trading began with a bit of desperation. What was it like for you?

Graham: That's not how I started. I've never traded in a sim. When I was getting started, I traded with real money. It was money that I lost that I could have saved by trading in a sim. When I got started, I was also a business owner, and I was making decent money. So I was like, "This might be something cool that I can try out. I can throw some money at it." It wasn't going to kill me if I lost $10,000 or $20,000.

Ross: That's definitely a different perspective. You had the benefit of income, so you didn't need to make money trading in those first couple of years.

> "...many people say, 'If you have money, you can make money.' But that's not what happened. I had money but was not making any money with it."

Graham: Yeah. My business was making me good money, so I could just take stabs at things. The funny part is, many people say, "If you have money, you can make money." But that's not what happened. I had money but was not making any money with it. In hindsight, I would rather have started with an education in day trading and less money, rather than just waste my money being in the market with no education.

Ross: It sounds like you had a period where you were spinning your wheels. I know you went through the classes as part of your turning point, but do you have a specific trade, or a specific period when you broke out of going sideways and started to actually ascend?

Graham: I'll see people online say, "I had a light bulb moment" or something similar. That's not what happened to me. I had losers and winners for a long time. In other words, I was inconsistent, and it was a long process of tightening up my losers. I learned how to tighten up my strategy. I was like, *All right, I see how Ross is doing it, I see how other people are doing it. Let me see if I can get dialed in better.* From there, it was just about keeping my losers to a minimum, and then starting to slowly increase my winners.

After you've been negative, at some point you look back and you're breakeven on the month. Many people are like, "Oh, that's frustrating." But I saw that as a good thing. After a while I looked back on the month, and I'm like, *Wow, I made 1,000 bucks!* And that's how it slowly started to grow.

After some more months, I realized, *Wow, I'm up 30 grand. I'm getting it.* From there, it was a matter of keeping my emotions in check, and keeping myself accountable for all those trades.

Ross: That's interesting that you had it that way. For me, there was definitely a rock bottom loss where I was like, *I just put my account way below the $25k Pattern Day Trader level, and now I've got to sell stuff in my barn on Craigslist to put more money in my account.* I was running out of stuff to sell.

I figured this was my last shot, because I'd accumulated a lot of credit card debt. I could take everything out of my trading account to pay it, but then my trading account would be gone. I chose to let things ride up on the credit card balance and keep the cash in the trading account. Then I lost more, and it was that final loss where I felt like I hit rock bottom. I was like, *It either turns around right now or you're done. You can't add more money.*

At that point, the stakes were pretty high, and it forced me to follow the rules in a way that was much more serious than what I had done before. I think that is common for some people. But what you experienced is also common, which is a slow transition from consistently losing—but not maybe getting crushed—to then treading water. That stage can last sometimes for years.

Then, a couple of months go by and you're like, *Whoa, my account balance is up by twenty, thirty grand.* That's when it started—at least for me—to get a little scary. It's almost like a fear of heights, because then, inevitably, you do have a loss. Do you have any memory of one of those first big losses and how you handled that?

Graham: Yeah, I was going up, and I was like, *I'm going to crush this next trade.* And I went right back to breakeven. I thought, *You just gave all that back, after all that effort.* That's when many people decide to quit. But I always looked at it as a chance to keep going, to get back up and try again. I figured I did it before, so why can't I do it again?

Ross: I think that we both have that fight instinct after a big loss to get right back in. It can border on revenge trading, when you start to get sloppy. I also think that we both have a hard time knowing when to walk away. We'll have days where it's like, *Dude, I was up $5,000, and now I'm down $5,000. How did this happen?*

Graham: Exactly.

Ross: Maybe a little of that is hard-wired, but I think some people have the opposite, where the pain of losing is so bad that they feel, *I can't possibly come back.*

I felt a little bit that way after losing $300,000 at one point. It was just like, *Oh my God, that amount is so big, I can't possibly come back tomorrow and just literally come in here to only make two grand.*

Graham: It's definitely interesting to see that, because, from the outside, people like me were looking at you and thinking, *It's really not that bad. Yeah, he lost a lot, but if you look at the big picture, he's still doing great.*

Ross: It's hard to have that outside perspective of, "Hey, you're still green overall."

So what do you do now when you have a big red day, or a red week, or whatever? How do you get yourself re-centered?

Graham: It's not as bad anymore. I can take maybe a six, seven, $8,000 loss, and be like, *All right, I'm done until tomorrow.* I can brush it off pretty well. It's maybe after I take a hit the next day, and then the day after that, where I think, *How do I break out of this?*

Ross: Back-to-back red days.

Graham: Yeah. Obviously, talking to someone about it helps, because other people are having the same situation that I have. But mostly what I like to do is I recenter, and I avoid setups that are high risk. I just go back to the basics, and that usually serves me the best. So I'll stick to a five-minute setup, or trade only stocks with maybe ten million shares of volume, or very high volume. That'll tend to set me straight. Once I do that, it's like, *All right, you're back in the game, now just keep that trend.*

Ross: For me, it's also getting back to basics. I think that sometimes when trading is going really well, it's easy to get a little complacent and to take higher-risk setups, because sometimes they pay off. Then, when you're struggling, it's like, *I really need to dial this back to my go-to setups that I have the most confidence in.*

On another topic, as you continue to trade, what's your goal in terms of scaling your strategy? Is there a part of you that's trying to stretch, or are you trying to just keep it nice and steady?

Graham: That's a great question. As traders, we can think about it in two ways. I can easily come in here every day and just say, "You know what? I'm going to take 1,000 shares, make whatever type of profit I'm looking for, and walk away." But as a trader, you also see the potential in the market, and you want to scale. You want to grow.

That's exactly what I've been doing: trading larger sizes, but also trying to take better trades, with more accuracy, and just all-around improve my trading. I used to trade 1,000 or 2,000 shares. Now, I'm up to maybe 8,000 or 10,000 on a hot day. I would like to actually scale up to maybe 25 or 30,000 shares eventually.

Ross: It's definitely possible. Certainly with a bigger size, you might not be able to get in and out as quickly. You might get five cents of slippage on the entry, you might get another five on the exit. So, what would have been twenty cents might only be ten. Maybe it's actually flat, maybe it's red. And, of course, with bigger sizes, you're going to have bigger losses. The thing that we've talked about quite a bit is emotional conditioning, and sizing up gradually.

Now, when you're planning a trade, what are you looking at specifically?

Graham: If I'm looking at a really nice trade, obviously my main focus is the chart. It's the chart, my moving averages, the price action, how the candles are working their way up to a pivot point or a breakout point or something like that. Then I can easily set my entry price, so I'm looking at a key level to get to the trade. As soon as I am ready to take that trade, I focus all my energy on the Level 2[24] and the Time and Sales window[25], because that's going to show what's going on. I want to see if lots of people are buying, or if no one's buying. I watch the price action on the chart, and that'll tell me if the trade's working in my favor, or hey, maybe it's time to stop out and look for a new entry.

Ross: I've noticed that sometimes you'll have a really good entry, and the stock will squeeze up and you take it off the table, and then it's consolidating and you're like, "I can't get back in up here." So what's that about? Because I usually will get back in. I mean, if it's genuinely very extended—we've got six green candles in a row—maybe I'll hesitate. But if it's just forming a new 1-minute setup, and it's just $2 a share higher, I don't have a problem buying it up there. But you sometimes seem to, so what's that about?

Graham: That's probably the main difference in our trading. You have no problem getting back in it, and more times than not, it works out. Whereas I think I've already had the perfect position, and then I've sold the stock. Now I'm thinking, *Why would I rebuy it higher than where I sold it? I already owned it at this price!* I think that has to do with my business background. It's something that's burned into me that I've been actually trying to work my way out of doing. I've been getting better at adding higher, and retaking a whole new position higher.

Ross: The strategy can work, but sometimes it can be a real problem, for sure. There are times where I'm back in and I had a good average at $35 a share. Then suddenly, I'm long full size at $48 a share, and it

---

[24] This is a key tool that shows trade details in real time.

[25] This is the so-called "tape" where you can see every order that goes through the market.

drops back down to $38. I'm like, *How did I get back in so high?* It's all about trying to have that presence of mind when I'm trading as it's going higher and higher to reduce my share size, and to not continue to trade with the same size I might have had when it was several dollars a share lower. That way, if I do lose, I'm at least not going to give back everything from that good entry.

Now, you have been a big advocate of trading in small accounts. With domestic brokers, a small account has to be at least $25,000 and realistically, you're probably going to keep it around $35k or $40k, which means you could buy $120,000 in stock. What's your thought process on working small accounts instead of bigger accounts?

Graham: When I started becoming an active day trader, I found that the small account really appealed to me, because I didn't have to lock up fifty grand in an account. Another thing that I found, which is a negative sort of trigger for me: if I have a $50,000 account, I'm trading and before I know it, I look down: I'm

"...when I trade in a smaller account, it keeps me mindful of the risk I'm taking, and it keeps me grounded."

maxed out on my buying power, I'm maxed out on my trading, and I'm just getting reckless. But when I trade in a smaller account, it keeps me mindful of the risk I'm taking, and it keeps me grounded.

Ross: It's a smart thing you do that. Through the GameStop period, I was using a full $2 million in buying power on some of those trades, which, given the stock price of $300, 3,000 shares is $900 grand. It didn't take that many shares to hit my buying power max.

Then I would have those moments where I was like, *I'm putting literally $2 million into this. What if, right now—the second I'm in—the exchange halts it? And they say, "We demand an answer from GameStop." And GameStop says "We have no news to account for this move", and it resumes at $50 a share? Or they say, "We're going to halt trading in it for a month"?*

None of that stuff happened. Some of that stuff is a fear of an imaginary outcome that's probably not likely, but there are some scary scenarios. A halt for a month is probably unlikely on a big stock like

GameStop, but a halt for a few hours, and then no news—that could have happened.

In the heat of the moment, I just kept pressing Shift +1[26], and suddenly, I'm now seeing max buying power. This is a lot of money on the line, and I sometimes feel like I can't really trust myself not to use the buying power when I have it. Because when I have it, I use it.

But you hear about people who do keep all their profits in their account and then go bigger and bigger. It can then be one trade that knocks it down by half. It's such a big loss, and the emotional damage is serious.

Graham: Yeah. I think you hit it perfectly. Say you lost most of your account because trading was halted. You'd be fine, but the emotional issues when trading the next day would be so great that you wouldn't even be trading with a strategy. You'd be trading out of just fear, thinking, *Oh my God, what if this one does it? Or what if the next one does it?*

But if that ever happened to me in a small account, I could just reload. It would never devastate me. It's like you are always saying, "You're rock climbing and you're setting your anchors higher and higher. If you fall, yeah, you fall, but is it going to kill you? No."

Ross: You're right. That's the thing with those big losses: it costs you not only the money of the loss, but it also costs you everything you lose in the coming weeks, because you're trading fearfully. You are nervous, you're not yourself, and it takes time to recover. Sometimes that can be the beginning of a downward spiral.

Of course, the worst timing would be that this happens at the peak of the market, and then it fades hard. Then the market stays choppy for weeks or months with no way to really make back those losses in a serious way, and you're just sitting with them.

That brings us to the head-space of trading. What percent of trading would you say is skill versus psychology?

Graham: I'd put more than half on psychology. Anyone can learn a strategy, but most won't have the mental strength to follow the rules of the strategy. It's such a strong mental game when you're trading

---

[26] My hotkey to buy.

> "Anyone can learn a strategy, but most won't have the mental strength to follow the rules of the strategy."

and you're feeling the emotion of profit and loss.

Especially when you're a new trader, you want to take the trade and you want to lock it in as fast as possible, because you don't want to experience a loss. So, you're taking those little one-cent winners or something like that. Then on the next one, you take the entry, and it flushes on you. So, you are capping your winners, and you get a big loser, and there's so much emotion behind that. It's what triggers you as a trader, whereas if you're completely robotic about it, it's better for you, to be honest.

Ross: How do you stay grounded when you have a day where you make 3,000 bucks, and then you go to the supermarket, and you can load up your entire grocery cart and not spend more than $300? You could be walking by people, thinking *I probably made more than every single one of you will make today.* How do you compartmentalize those gains, stay grounded, and not lease the Lamborghini?

Graham: I've done the opposite. I'll think, *I just lost $11,000 today. I could have bought quite a bit of stuff with that. I could have given that to someone who needed it.* You don't even want to go down that road mentally.

Ross: You don't want to do the math of how many cups of coffee or how many $6.78 bags of dried pineapple I could have bought with that.

Graham: It's definitely hard to do. The best thing for anyone that experiences that is you got to look at what you're actually doing overall. You need to look at the gains as well as the losses, because they'll bring you back to reality. The gains and the losses will keep you grounded, for sure.

Ross: Do you ever feel trading is addictive and hard to walk away from? Both in the sense of an individual day, but even in the big picture? Let's say you made a lot of money in one year. Could you just say, "I'm done. I'm going to stop." Could you ever actually stop?

Graham: No, I could not. If someone handed me a bunch of money so that I didn't have to work another day in my life, I would still be trading. I have a deep interest in the markets and in trading. It's the financial reward, but it's also my gamer background where I enjoy making the proper setups, and being right.

Ross: The gratification.

Graham: Yeah, exactly.

Ross: It's a sense of fulfillment. We haven't created something physical, but we've achieved, we solved the puzzle, we've passed the level.

> "If someone handed me a bunch of money so that I didn't have to work another day in my life, I would still be trading."

Graham: Exactly.

Ross: Every day that you get that, you get a little dopamine reward of another good day. And after a bad day, on the next good day, it's then contrasted and you feel so much better.

So, tell me a little about your mentoring experience, because you've been helping to mentor others. For a long time I've said that teaching can make people better traders. What has your experience been, now that you've begun to teach and mentor?

Graham: It's been really rewarding in a non-financial way, because I see other people saying, "Hey, you made me mindful to maybe try this," or "You pointed something out that I didn't see, and it turned my trading around." That's a big reward for me, because now they can provide for their family, or this becomes their newfound passion. And maybe that will spread to someone else.

On top of that, I'm much more mindful of my own trading. A lot of it is, *Do I want to be held accountable for this terrible trade? Do I want to take this super high-risk trade so I can beat my chest and say, "Here's my big winner"?* No, I want to show what I did, and provide a good education to someone who wants to learn that type of setup.

Ross: What you said about accountability is big. For me, posting my brokerage statements means I don't sweep losers under the carpet. So if I have a big loss, or I do something stupid, I'm definitely going to be talking about it. That encourages me to second-guess myself a little, like, *Is this really the right one?* I still make mistakes sometimes and have a preventable or oversized loss. Then I talk about it. And that accountability system is important.

It's a good idea for everyone to find a way to be held accountable. Before I was teaching and mentoring, I didn't have a friend with an interest in trading, so I paid someone to go over my trades with me once a week. It's possible to do this arrangement with some type of life coach, or counselor, or someone like that. To me it was money well spent, because I had to create an accountability system. It went beyond just knowing the rules of the strategy.

I still struggle with that. At this point, it's so easy for me to think, *I've made enough money. I clearly know what I'm doing. I don't have to be accountable to someone else.* But I keep doing it because accountability is really important, both as a beginner, but even for where I'm at.

I'm curious if there is any setup that you really strongly avoid, like a biggest loser. Something where you're just like, "I will never trade that again"?

Graham: Yeah. The GameStop type of stock is burned into me now, because I couldn't get a read on it. You had a read on it and you were trading it, but a lot of times when those stocks are just whipping around ten points, I'm like, *I don't know if I can read this.* If I can't make sense of it, I'm definitely avoiding those types of setups.

Ross: That's a good approach. Do you have any last words of wisdom to share with someone getting started?

Graham: Yeah. First, when you're getting started, cut your losses. Cut your losses *quickly.* Do not average down on a terrible position! You're doing yourself a disservice if you try to maneuver as the stock is falling. Other than that, I think self-belief is the key. You've got to believe in yourself and what you're doing, and how hard what you're doing actually is. So give yourself some time. If you lose a little, it's part of it. Losing is part of trading.

Ross: That's absolutely right. It's a learning curve. Okay, thank you, Graham!

Graham: Thanks for having me. I'm glad we could talk about all this stuff.

"...when you're getting started, cut your losses. Cut your losses quickly."

CHAPTER 13

Interview with Martin

Ross: This interview is with Martin,[27] who is a million-dollar badge holder at Warrior.[28] So let's talk a little about your experience of learning to trade. How long have you been trading?

Martin: I've been trading for three full years. I spent the first eight months or so in the simulator. Since then, I've been live, and it's been about two and a half years of live trading.

Ross: So eight months in a sim before you went live?

Martin: Yes, I know that is a lot, but there's a backstory why that happened. I really wanted to invest some money that I had in an IRA account, but it was controlled by my parents, who had some bad experiences in the stock market, and they warned me against it. My dad had taken a few thousand dollars and turned it into more than $100,000. But he didn't take any of those profits and in the end, he lost money on it.

Ross: I have talked with a lot of people who have struggled with this issue of not having much family support when they got into trading. And not just family support, but from friends too. When people are in the earliest phases of exploring trading, it may be better to keep it a bit more to themselves until they have a little more confidence. But I know you couldn't do that if they controlled the IRA.

Martin: Looking back at it, honestly I think of it as a blessing in disguise. Because I was trading in the sim and because I was profitable, I

---

[27] Note: I have changed the name of this person in order to respect his privacy.

[28] Martin's trading results should not be considered typical, or an indication of a result you should expect.

could show them regular updates on what I was doing. After about the sixth time of discussing it, I just said, "Hey, I really want to do this" and they said OK.

Ross: One important thing about trading in a sim is that it helps give you a track record. And that track record is good not only for your own sense of confidence, but it can also be something that's helpful to show someone else whom you want to have on board supporting you—maybe a spouse or someone else whose opinion matters.

So you've been trading for three full years, but let's back up a little. Did you grow up with stock market investors in the family?

Martin: Not at all. Around high school, I was on Twitter and on Instagram. I was looking at all these kids who said they were making like hundreds of thousands of dollars. I thought, *Wow, that's crazy. I want to turn some money into a lot of money.* So I started taking just small amounts of money — I was a junior in high school — and I was putting it in Robinhood.

I thought I had a strategy of buying stocks that were gapping down 40 or 50 percent on the day. I wanted to buy those to swing them into overnight trades. I thought they were at a discount, so they'd go up, eventually. But that wasn't the case, and that account just never worked out for me.

Ross: You went to college, right?

Martin: Yes I did.

Ross: What was your focus in college?

Martin: I had no idea what I wanted to do. I went to Illinois State University and majored in business administration. After two years, COVID hit.

Therefore, the second half of my college career was actually spent online. But because I realized it was going to be continued online, I transferred to an online school where I could choose my schedule and graduate a lot sooner for a lot less money.

I went to Purdue Global University for the last two years. That also really benefited my trading schedule, which is another reason I did that, and that was super beneficial for me.

Ross: Yeah, that makes sense. I don't know to what extent you need a college degree to be a day trader. But I think the perseverance of getting a degree and finishing it is a good character trait. It's a good indicator of someone who wants to get something and see it through. I also had that mentality with college. I finished it not because I really believed it was going to benefit me, but because it was half done. I felt that I needed to see it through. This may not be even a good thing.

Martin: Yeah, totally. And now, at least I have a degree where that's something to fall back on, but hopefully it won't ever come to that.

Ross: Absolutely. So what were you doing before you started trading? Were you ever working a regular job or were you working in college?

Martin: No, I never had a real job, and I was always a full-time student. But in the summers, I worked at a golf course as a groundskeeper, and one summer I worked at a law firm in the city. That was a cool experience, but it never really came to be a real job.

Ross: In terms of what brought you to trading, it sounds like it was social media and a little FOMO, seeing other people flaunting some trading success, right?

Martin: Yes. And also some of my friends and I had actually talked about it years ago. But after that Robinhood account didn't do well, I kind of put it to the side.

Then a couple of years went by. The reason that I got back into it was because I heard some of my friends were back in and making 1 percent or 2 percent a day in their account. I thought, *Wow, that's crazy.* At first when I heard that, I was like, "You guys are going to give back all your money. Day trading is stupid. It's a scam."

But after I heard about their success, I thought, *OK, if they're doing it, I think I can do it too.* So I got back into it, and it's kind of because of them that I'm actually trading now.

Ross: That's interesting. That's very similar to me in the sense that I graduated during the Great Recession, so the job market wasn't great. I was living in Vermont and thinking about what I could do from home. My memory of a friend who had done well in the market made me look at investing to see if it was an option.

So did you consider anything else before trading? You mentioned the law office.

Martin: At first it sparked my interest a little, but once I got into it, I realized it was not for me in the long run. One thing I really wanted to get into, though, and that had been a long-time interest of mine, was I really wanted to be a real estate investor. I didn't know how I would get there, but I figured that some way, somehow, I would eventually.

"...trading has given me the freedom of time and also financial freedom."

Fortunately, trading has given me the freedom of time and also financial freedom. It's allowing me to look into real estate investing after all.

Ross: That makes sense with the profits that you're making. Speaking of profits, some people say to me, "Ross, you should just keep collecting your profits in your account, and just go bigger and bigger." Other people agree with what I actually do, which is to keep my trading account relatively small. I take most profits out and reinvest them in other things. What has been your approach?

Martin: Yeah, that's my approach, too. It depends on the market that we're in, but I like to keep my trading account around $200,000, which is obviously a lot larger than other people can go. But it gives me the freedom—when there's a stock that's really moving—to take a lot of share size and potentially profit on it quite a bit.

I keep my other money in a separate account. Eventually, I want to invest in other things. It's one of my goals for this year.

Ross: That you're not keeping all of it in the account is a good risk management technique. You are not allowing yourself to be in a situation where you could take a multimillion dollar position and in the heat of the moment, suddenly have one day where everything is thrown out the window.

Martin: Exactly.

Ross: What has been the biggest surprise for you about learning how to trade or about trading in general?

Martin: I'd seen people making a lot of money online, but I was surprised at

"I was surprised at how profitable it really could be with a regular strategy like ours. Of course, it's also super risky, and you can lose the amount that you make."

how profitable it really could be with a regular strategy like ours. Of course, it's also super risky, and you can lose the amount that you make.

But I was surprised, because going into it, I thought I would be lucky to double my account in a year, and I did well over that the first year. So yeah, I was beyond surprised that I could do that.

Ross: What role have emotions played in your success as a trader? Do you feel like that's something you struggle with—trading psychology—or is that something that comes naturally to you?

Martin: I was an athlete growing up, and one thing that I could always do well is understand that losses are going to happen. It's how you react to those losses that shows what your success is going to be.

However, I still have days where I take one red trade and I'm like, *Oh, man, I just lost a lot.* And I decide to do just one more trade. Then I lose more. And I'm like, *Okay, I can make it back,* and I do another trade. I then just keep digging a deeper hole. That's something I've been struggling with even this year. I'm having a lot bigger losses and not managing them as well as I should be.

There definitely are some moments that I see negative thoughts go through my mind and they can spiral out of control.

Ross: That happened to me early in my career, and in those days, it was desperation and frustration. Then I got it under control for quite a while, and it kind of came back after I had a couple of really good years.

I think it was a bit of overconfidence, like, *I know I can make this back. I've made it back on other days.* I was getting really stubborn and my ego got involved. It absolutely doesn't feel good to lose.

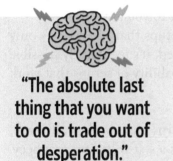

"The absolute last thing that you want to do is trade out of desperation."

Martin: A couple of days ago, you said something about trading out of desperation, just trying to make any win. And on some days, I feel like I'm just trading out of desperation. That's when I have my worst days. The absolute last thing that you want to do is trade out of desperation.

Ross: On days when the market's hot, if you hit your goal very early on, you're not going to be nearly as aggressive as you are on one of those red days, because you don't feel the need to be trying to squeeze blood out of a rock. You don't need to push it.

That creates for me the effect of amplifying on the red days and not maximizing on the green days.

Martin: That's something that I struggle with a lot, too. I put way too much time and effort into the days that I'm red, when I should do that on the days that are green.

I'm also proud of myself this year, because I've been getting out of the market really early and not giving myself the chance to go red on my green days. In the past, I struggled with going from green to red and really red. This year I'm not giving myself the opportunity to do that and I just get out early.

Ross: You're in a place where you've had quite a bit of success and so it can be very easy to give in to those feelings of frustration and try to push a little harder, because in the past you've been able to recoup those losses. But you've also had a few of those really big drawdowns, and you know how frustrating it is to be in them. That's certainly motivation to avoid doing that again.

What is something that other traders do—maybe beginners or

even experienced traders—that you just shake your head, where you're like, *Wow, that is so reckless.*

Martin: One thing that comes to mind is people who are always out for themselves in trading. They don't want to share anything about what they do. This sounds a little funny, but I think that if more people know how you trade, I see it as a benefit to you as well.

That's because if more people see the setups that you see, it's only going to create more success for you. Granted, it's technically possible to crowd a stock. But there is a higher probability of setups that work out for you.

Ross: That's interesting. If you have patterns that work really well, the more people that see those patterns, it's a self-fulfilling prophecy. VWAP works well because so many people see it and respect it. If you're getting really good at recognizing a pattern, it seems like it makes sense to share those ideas and say, "Hey, guys, there's a stock here that looks good. I'm not the only one that sees this, right?"

> "...if more people see the setups that you see, it's only going to create more success for you."

It's both reaffirming when other people are like, "Yeah, I see it. I like it too." But it's also helpful if someone says, "No, the 200 moving average is right there," or they have some other reason. And then you're like, "Right, good thought. I didn't see that."

I think that shows both the benefit of trading in a community and also the drawback of trading where you're isolated, because you can get a confirmation bias without having anyone to test your theory.

Martin: Definitely. That's been the positive side of being in Warrior. Just the other day I typed into the chat that there's a pattern that I like. And exactly like you said, someone pointed out a technical indicator, and I was like, "Okay, yeah, you're right. I don't really care for this trade anymore."

Ross: Who do you think is not suited to be a day trader?

"...someone pointed out a technical indicator, and I was like, "Okay, yeah, you're right. I don't really care for this trade anymore."

Martin: First off, I kind of hit on it a little earlier, which is people who can't learn from their losses. You're going to have losses as a trader. If people say that they haven't lost in years, they're wrong. Everyone has red days. Everyone has red trades. No matter what, if you're a trader, you're going to take losses. It's a matter of how you understand those and move on from them to get better.

Every day is a challenge, and every day you're looking to improve your strategy as a trader. People that don't do that are not set up to succeed. I also think that people who are not patient enough to either wait for the setups, or to go in the sim for long enough, should not trade.

I was in the simulator for eight months. If I had to do it over again, I would do the same thing. It was the best thing for me. It created a sense of patience for myself, and I think that has benefited my trading massively.

Ross: Yeah, patience. That is big. And that ties into discipline, too, because it's having the discipline to hold that patience when other people are getting impatient. Impatience is a symptom of someone who's not very disciplined.

Martin: One thing I want to hit on, too, is what I saw when I went to the Warrior All-Star Summit. Those people were some of the more profitable traders in the chat room, and I realized just how disciplined every one of those people was. I thought I was super disciplined in what I did, but these people took it to another level.

"Discipline is an absolutely massive key for being successful in the stock market."

They're up at the same time. Some of them don't even drink coffee until after they're done trading. They go to the gym every single morning. Discipline is an absolutely massive key for being successful in the stock market.

Ross: I agree with that. And it's something that I struggle with at times. I don't want anyone listening to just assume, *Oh, wow, these guys must just be super disciplined naturally, like they were born with it.* I think that for all of us, it's sometimes a struggle.

Being disciplined can become a habit and it can become a way of life, but it doesn't mean that it's fun every day, or that it's easy. We just have the understanding that there is no other way to get through this market except to be disciplined. For lack of any other choice, we hold it together. Other people underestimate how important that is and cannot do it themselves.

Martin: Right. For people with a typical job, let's say they go to bed late because they were out drinking or whatever. The next day, of course they can get through, even if they're slow. But for us, if we're not on our A game, we can lose a lot. We can lose our shirts.

Ross: I have a friend who has a government job. He watches Netflix about half the day on his computer because he's got his own sort of little cubicle. He's been at this job for eight years, maybe longer, and he just phones it in and keeps getting his paycheck. But you can't do that with trading. If you want to get something out of it, you've got to put in a lot.

Martin: Absolutely.

Ross: So who would you say is perhaps best suited to be a trader?

Martin: That's a tricky question. We've hit on traits that a lot of bad traders have, and things like discipline that good traders have. Something that I would look for in a person is adaptability. It's something that we absolutely need to have for both hot and cold markets.

I wouldn't even consider myself to be the best at it, either. Going from a hot market to a cold market, that's where I take my biggest losses, thinking, *Hey, this market is still hot. I'll continue to push with maximum share size.*

Again, even if you acquire those traits, it does not mean that you're going to be a successful trader even a little, until you put in the effort and the time.

Ross: I agree for sure. Someone could have the aptitude that might make them more likely to be successful, but they're still not successful for a variety of other reasons. Then other people may not really have the aptitude, but then they actually pull it together and find success.

Switching gears, did you try other systems or learn from other people before you settled in with me? And if you did, how would you contrast your experience with me versus somebody else?

Martin: You're the only course that I ever bought. But for the first two months of my trading journey, until I found you, I was kind of focusing on large caps and ETFs and just trying to find the major support levels and stuff like that. I didn't find success in that. I would make $1,000 today, and lose $1,000 the next day. This was in a sim, as I said, and I kept going back and forth. I had red day, green day, red day, green day, and never found consistent success.

One thing that's a lot different between day traders and typical large-cap and ETF traders is that day traders hold for much less time. We're in and out. I mean, I think my average trade time is under two minutes and yours is longer. Some of these large-cap traders hold for fifteen, twenty, thirty minutes or longer.

Ross: It's a different strategy, for sure. Were there any times where you thought maybe trading wasn't going to work out for you?

Martin: Yeah. Within the first week that I actually put real money into the account. On the first day I made $200, and then the next day I lost $2,000. At the time, my account was about $28,000. Losing that $2,000 put me down to $26,000. I was like, *Down $2,000. That's a lot of freaking money for me.*

I was a full-time student then, so that was more than I made in a month. That was when I started to contemplate it, and it was tough.

Ross: So what kept you going?

Martin: The ability to look back at my trading profits through the sim was the biggest key to it, as well as talking through my thoughts and feelings. My girlfriend was a really big part of this, actually. We have been together for almost ten years now, and she helped me to understand exactly what I was feeling. She would say things like, "OK, well, you know what? You're not going to get better at trading if you don't get back up and push yourself to do better." She also reminded me of my success in the sim and gave me more confidence.

"You're not going to get better at trading if you don't get back up and push yourself to do better."

Ross: That's awesome. Yeah. I was talking to my wife the other night because I have a 1961 Volkswagen bus, and I've been having this continual problem with it. It's very difficult to start. I said that I felt like I should bring it to someone, but these are such old cars, I didn't know who to bring it to. She was quick to point out, "Aren't those the simplest engines to work on?"

I was like, No, you're right. I can figure this out myself. And you know what? I got out there and did get it figured out.

Sometimes it's easy to sell yourself short and think, *I'm not going to figure this out.* And someone needs to give you a little kick and say, "I think you could do this."

Martin: For sure. Having that kind of mutual support from somebody else to remind you of your past successes, that's extremely powerful. Definitely a big factor for why I was successful.

Ross: If you were going to start over, is there anything that you would do differently?

Martin: Actually, I would have bought your course a little sooner, because I had traded in the sim and it was about a year before I got your course. But another thing is I would have sized down my Sim account to be closer to what I would have when trading with real money. Instead, I was trading with up to $600,000 in the Sim account.

Ross: That's a great observation. One of the biggest drawbacks of simulated trading is it doesn't replicate liquidity realities in the market. You can punch a buy order in a simulator for 100,000 shares, even when in the real market there's only 100 shares for sale. So I'm an advocate of trying to treat a sim like real money by using just 1,000 shares. I also measure performance in a sim not as much based on total dollars of profit, but on consistency of average cents per share that you're pulling out of the market. If you can do that consistently with 100 shares, you could probably do it with 1,000, or 2,000.

So you said earlier that you dealt with some resistance from your parents. What was the feedback you were getting from other people when you were starting?

Martin: There wasn't much feedback. People didn't really understand what trading was, and especially my strategy. When I got successful, people would say, "Can I give you some money so you can make me this return in this amount of time?" I'd say, "No, that's just not possible because it's not how it works." Trading was my full-time job, and I'd be taking myself away from my job to trade that money, and I would miss my own opportunities.

> " I also measure performance in a Sim not as much based on total dollars of profit, but on consistency of average cents per share that you're pulling out of the market."

Ross: I've had many people ask me that, too. I understood where they were coming from. Some people had tried trading, knew how hard it was, and were like, "Can you just trade this money for me?" Others had no interest in trading, but had some extra money. I had to explain that trading has a limit to scalability and at some point, the amount that we make is not based on how much is in the account. It's based on the particular opportunity in the market.

Martin: Exactly. But speaking of how people think about trading, I had an uncle who asked me if I was ever going to get a real job or if I was just going to continue to bum around. I guess many people think of day traders as bums.

Ross: Yeah, some people have the belief that trading isn't a real job. All they see is you are just punching keys on a keyboard. It's especially strange for someone who might be more used to a traditional 9:00 to 5:00 job.

About what you said earlier was one of your biggest surprises, it is incredible how quickly you can make or lose $5,000 in one day trading. It takes a tremendous amount of time and dedication before you get to the place where you can actually find any consistency with locking up those opportunities and turning them into profit.

Martin: Exactly.

Ross: When you look back at your first three years now in the market, are there any turning points?

> "I had an uncle who asked me if I was ever going to get a real job or if I was just going to continue to bum around. I guess many people think of day traders as bums."

Martin: I would say the first turning point was finding you and finding a consistent, profitable strategy. Outside of that, once I had actually gone live out of the sim, the first month I was down about $5,600. The next month I made back $5,500 of that. So I was going into the new year pretty much with a clean slate, down like $100 overall. But then in January I made $10,000. I thought, *Holy cow, I know it's not realistic, but if I were to do that for the next eleven months of the year, I'd have $120,000 and I'm in college. I'd be making six figures in college.*

That was just crazy to me. It was at that point that I realized the possibility of day trading. So then the next month I made $36,000, which I thought was like, *Holy cow.* The month after, I made over $100,000.

It was in those first three months after getting out of the sim that I realized what trading could be. I had known it could be profitable, but I didn't think it would happen the way that it did.

I don't think I have any turning point that I can give advice on, in the sense of "I did X, Y, and Z." But I think there's a theme with a lot of experienced traders where it was about learning one thing after another. Eventually it just kind of fed into a profitable strategy where we could be consistent and profitable.

Ross: Yeah. Someone put it eloquently: "It's just about sucking a little less each day."

Martin: That's perfect.

Ross: There is truth to that. Through the process of trading in a sim, you get quick feedback on what's working and what's not working.

If you are starting from a place of taking something like my strategy, which works very well for me, and you're trying to implement it, you look closely at: *What's Ross doing? What am I doing? Where is the disconnect? When he's green, I'm red. What did I do wrong?* Then when we're both green, okay, that's good. Then when you have a big loss, you can quickly look at, *What did I do wrong here?*

You take that loss, turn it into a lesson, and learn from it. Not every time you have a loss is going to be a learning lesson. Some losses are small and are just part of trading. And you came into the market at a really strong time, for sure.

> "It's just about sucking a little less each day."

Martin: I did, yeah. 2021 was definitely a good year.

Ross: One takeaway for traders who are reading this is the fact that you can't control that you didn't start a year earlier, but as soon as you make the commitment to learn trading, you should try to gain as much experience as you can.

If you're learning during a period that's hot, you don't know how long that window will stay open. And if you're learning during a period that's cold, then you've got a little runway to spend time studying to get ready for when it does heat back up.

Many people don't come into the market until it's hot. That's just how human psychology is, that when things are hot, that's when people come into it. If you're someone who's already into it before it heats up, you're better able to capitalize on that full window of good momentum, which will happen when the market turns around.

Martin: Absolutely. And I do think even if you're starting to learn during a cold market, one positive that you can take out of it is that it's a lot easier to learn good habits then. You're going to be more punished in the bad periods, so you have to be more disciplined. In order to survive in a cold market, you must stay disciplined. It's a matter of surviving through the cold market to get to the hot market, where then you can really thrive.

Ross: So what does your day look like as a trader right now? Run me through your typical day.

Martin: My alarms are set for 5:30 and 5:45. I'm on Pacific time. I usually get to the computer by about 6:00 a.m. I spend about half an hour looking through the watch list, seeing what I like, and just getting my leading gappers.

I'll also get my coffee then. Lately I've been done by about 8:30 Pacific time. I'll then go get breakfast and head to the gym. After that, I don't really think about trading for the rest of the day.

One thing that's been successful for me is that I can just be done with my day and not really think about it. Of course, the red days can stick around through my thoughts, but I like to do things to get my mind off of it. I'll go out in the yard and play with the dog, just to get away from my thoughts of trading. I think it's important to move on and take each day for what it is, and not really think about your previous day.

"In order to survive in a cold market, you must stay disciplined. It's a matter of surviving through the cold market to get to the hot market, where then you can really thrive."

Ross: That's interesting. I sometimes find that on a red day, what I might want to do for the rest of the day changes a bit. On other days, I might do gardening or yard work. Those are tasks where you can spend a lot of time in your thoughts, and they can be relaxing and meditative. But if I do them on a red day, and I have intrusive thoughts about this stupid trade I just took, they're not enjoyable.

So on red days, what I actually need are more of the activities that require a lot of focus, like downhill skiing, riding my mountain bike on a difficult trail in the woods, or playing tennis, because those are things where that activity becomes my focus. It forces the negative thoughts about my trading day to go to the back burner, because I just can't think about both at the same time.

Usually I find that when I'm done with that activity and that thought comes back, the time I've had to let it simmer on the back burner has given me the ability to gain some perspective and be like, You know what? It's not really a big deal.

But it can be very hard to not fall into the habit of just sitting and dwelling in your thoughts, which can make the lows of being a trader feel much lower than they need to be.

Martin: Having a hobby is super important to me. Something I can turn to when I'm having a bad day in trading, just to escape my thoughts.

I like golf, although it's one of the most frustrating sports I've ever played, because it's a personal sport, so it's all on me. But I do like it, so if I have a bad day, I often just go to the driving range. Or it might be something as simple as walking the dog.

Ross: Okay, so you're on Pacific time. What time do you try to go to bed each night?

Martin: If I'm not in bed by 10:00, I'm not going to have a good day. I won't wake up and be rejuvenated. I like to be in bed a little earlier and then have that time to unwind and fall asleep by 10:15 or 10:30 Anything later than 10:30, and I'm going to be a little cranky the next day.

"Having a hobby is super important to me. Something I can turn to when I'm having a bad day in trading, just to escape my thoughts."

Ross: What would you say are the best and worst aspects of day trading for you?

Martin: The best part about day trading, of course, is the financial freedom, but also the freedom of time. I'm done with my workday on Phoenix time by 8:30. That's basically the time that most people are just getting to work. The fact that I have the rest of the day to do whatever I want, it's crazy. It's insane. Also to have the ability to make more money than most people. When I was starting, I couldn't even dream of making this amount of money by this age. So it's really just crazy.

But the worst part of trading is all the emotions that you go through, and all the stress that you put yourself through. Like I said, recently I had three red months in a row. I put so much stress on myself just to get back to green, just to dig myself out of the hole, and I was trading out of desperation. So many emotions were running through my head.

Red day after red day. It was not fun. If you're looking to get into trading, it's going to put you through a lot of emotions that I never thought that I could even experience. But if you can handle that and become profitable, the freedom of time has been the absolute best part about it.

Ross: I certainly agree with you on both. One thing that you'll benefit from as you gain a bit more experience in your career is that you'll have more confidence in yourself, and you'll get through those red streaks faster. In anyone's career as a trader, when you hit your first couple of big drawdowns, you have a fear that puts questions in your head like: *Was my success to this point just luck? Do I actually know what I'm doing? Because right now, I feel like I don't.*

In your case, you might also think: *What kind of regular job am I going to get after having made this much money trading? Have I made enough that I could just retire at age 23?*

Martin: Just like you said, when I was over a million dollars in profits, I was like, *Okay, well, should I look for a job?* That was even after the time when I had clearly enough profits to fall back on. But it's just thinking about what to do if my three red months turn into more red months. That is not going to be good. What got me through it was the ability to stick through a cold market in order to get to the hot market.

Ross: What would you say for a beginner trader would be your biggest piece of advice?

Martin: One thing that really worked for me is sticking to the simulator to be patient and learn a profitable strategy before going live. Many people might not find that super helpful because it's not necessarily the same emotions that you're going to get through real trading.

However, if you have consistency in the sim and you have a proven profitable strategy, that's why you trade. You must have a profitable strategy. If you don't have that going into live trading, what are you doing? Otherwise, there's no point in trading, and you're setting yourself up for failure.

Ross: If you can't make money in a simulator, you have no business trading real money. You could argue that a sim is a little easier, because it doesn't replicate certain things. That's all the more reason to say that if you can't make money in the sim, do not trade with real money. The fact is, you can save yourself a lot of heartache, frustration, and unnecessary losses if you just put trading with real money on hold until you get things dialed in by using the sim.

> "One thing that really worked for me is sticking to the simulator to be patient and learn a profitable strategy before going live."

You can also explore multiple strategies that way. If one doesn't work for you, there's another one that might work.

Well, thank you for doing this interview!

Martin: Thank you. My pleasure.

CHAPTER 14

Next

I HAVE TO CONGRATULATE YOU: you've made it through this whole book, which was not some "easy money" promise, but instead a candid description of the skill and discipline necessary to become a day trader.

I also envy you. What I wouldn't have given for a guide like this when I started out! Nothing even remotely like it existed, and I shudder to think of the money and stress I could have avoided, had there been one.

I also envy the environment you're starting in. Technology has come so far in the past decade that it takes a lot of the manual drudgery out of trading. Notice that I didn't say it made day trading "easy"; it's just that now we have more of a high-resolution picture of the markets, rather than some grainy, narrow view.

In addition, the markets have never been more accessible than they are today. And one of the great things is that you don't even need an account or a ton of money to start learning. You know my advice is to trade in a sim before you put real money on the line. You can do that for free right now with many brokers.

I told you at the beginning of this book that I'm going to be as truthful as I know how to be, about what it takes to day trade. So allow me to be truthful about something else: I'd love to see you over at my trading community called Warrior Trading. We are by no means the only game in town. You have far more choices than I ever did for where you get your trading education, tools, and community.

You can take what I've given you in this book and go off to be a trader wherever you choose. The lessons I shared in this book are agnostic. You can use any trading tools or be part of whatever community you'd like.

Even so, I hope you'll check us out and see if we're a good fit for what you're after. If you go here[29] and leave your contact information, two things will happen:

    1. I will respect your privacy and will never sell or give your

---

[29] https://www.warriortrading.com/bookbonus/

contact info to anyone else; and

2. I'll send you a package of additional materials that I could not fit into this book. That's the beauty of the age we live in—it's so easy to deliver information electronically and instantly.

No matter what you decide, thank you for reading this book and thinking about maybe—just maybe—becoming a day trader.

CHAPTER 15

Glossary

HAVE YOU HAD THE FOLLOWING EXPERIENCE? You're reading about a complicated area that you know very little about, but would like to understand it better. You're a few pages in, and read about a few terms that are new to you. Then another bunch, then a whole lot of jargon. At this point it's really easy to close that book or browser window, never to return to it.

One of my biggest challenges in this book is to not overwhelm even really smart people with all there is to cover about day trading. Anyone's brain—mine for sure—can only soak up so much new material before no more gets in.

What seems like a completely different language will get clearer to you by the day, if you just hang in there. Here are some of the most-important terms for you to know.

Ask. Also called "offer." This is the lowest amount that current sellers on an exchange are willing to sell their shares for. Keep in mind that just because you see an ask price, it does not mean that you'll get that price when you actually hit the Buy button, for a whole variety of reasons. The difference between what you thought you *want to* pay and what you *end up* paying is called "slippage."

Bag holder. You don't want to be called this. It refers to someone who holds onto a stock position when it goes against them such that they have large losses. A big part of day trading involves avoiding this situation.

Bias. As in "short bias" and "long bias." If you have a short bias, you prefer to trade as stocks drop. That's fine as long as you are an experienced trader, you fully understand the risks, and you can absorb the consequences of being wrong, which WILL happen at least occasionally. Even though I understand those risks and can absorb the downside, I have a long bias. That doesn't make me "right" but it fits with my trading style.

Bid. This is the highest price that prospective buyers are willing to pay for a share of stock on a given exchange. Keep in mind that there are many exchanges, and they differ somewhat in the prices they show. Just as with the ask price, you may not get the bid price when you hit the Sell button, because actual trades are executed in tiny fractions of a second and the market may have moved between when you clicked, and when your order was executed.

Breakout. This is when a stock moves quickly above or below a significant support or resistance level, after failing to do so in previous attempts.

Buy the dip. This is a basic concept in day trading. It's where you buy a stock when it has dropped in price, and when you think it will soon rise in price, based on factors present at the moment.

Candlesticks. This is at the heart of day trading. It's a graphical representation of how the price of a stock has varied over a certain period. You can display candlesticks that represent ten seconds, or one minute, or one day, among many others. Once you get accustomed to interpreting candlesticks, they become an extremely fast way to get a sense of how a stock has moved.

Catalyst. Some sort of event that results in above-average interest in a stock by traders and investors. It might be breaking news, an earnings announcement, or other events.

Circuit breakers. These are relatively new mechanisms put in place at stock exchanges to halt trading if there is panic selling or other huge declines in stocks in a short period. The first circuit breaker was put into place after the Dow Jones Industrial Average dropped nearly 23 percent on October 19, 1987.

Commodities. Many tangible objects are traded as commodities, like gold, cotton, orange juice, and crude oil. The trading unit of commodities is the "futures contract," which is a bet on what the commodity will be worth in the future. This sort of trading is very different from what I teach, and I don't trade them. I might trade a gold ETF, but that's a stock and not a futures contract.

Cost basis. There is more than one meaning for this term, and they can get technical. The definition I'm referring to is your *average* cost of a stock position you take. Let's say you buy 100 shares at $10. Your cost basis is $10. But if the stock goes down to $9 and you buy another 100 shares, the cost basis for those shares is $9, but the cost basis of your overall position is $9.50.

Crypto. Cryptocurrencies like Bitcoin and Ethereum are digital currencies. They use a system called "blockchain" which involves much more than just currencies. I do not teach crypto trading, because it's enough to stick to small-cap stocks.

DJIA. Dow Jones Industrial Average. This is a mathematical calculation of the prices of thirty big companies that are listed on stock exchanges in the United States. It started in 1885 with thirty industrial stocks, but now contains decidedly non-industrial companies like Microsoft, Goldman Sachs, and Salesforce.

Day trader. My definition of a day trader is someone who focuses on chart patterns and technical analysis and does not hold positions overnight". That is in contrast to investors, who focus more on the longer-term fundamentals of a stock. I also define day traders as hunters of volatility and managers of risk.

Direct access routing. This is a type of system that allows direct access to a market; in other words, not through a broker. This can be crucial to day traders trying to get orders executed as quickly as possible. Direct access usually involves paying higher commissions for the benefit of that speed. Direct access routing isn't something that beginners need, but it will become useful after they've honed their skills over time.

Downtick. If a stock downticks, it goes lower in price than the last transaction.

Drawdown. This is a measurement, expressed as a percentage, from a peak in your account balance to what you currently have. It can be measured from your all-time peak in the account, or from a peak in a certain period like the current year.

Entry. This is the price at which you take a trade. You've calculated your risk/reward ratio and are taking a position in the stock, in line with your guardrails.

ETF. Exchange-Traded Funds. These are portfolios of stocks that focus on specific areas or industries. One ETF might contain hundreds or even thousands of stocks relating to environmental issues, or an industry like high-tech, and so on. Unlike mutual funds which usually are actively managed by a fund manager, ETFs are passive baskets of stocks.

FOMO. This is exactly what you think it is: Fear of Missing Out. It's a major influence on even seasoned day traders. Of course it's valid and important to participate in a stock that's going up and up, but it must be done within the trading parameters you establish up front. Otherwise FOMO can hijack your emotions and often result in buying at the top and giving back whatever gains you may have had.

Flash crash. This is when the HFT or computer-based trading systems go haywire and create huge swings in the price of some stocks. In 2010, one stock went from $41 per share to $0.01 per 100 shares in seventeen minutes. Other stocks went crazy as well.[30]

Float. This is an important measure of how many shares are available to trade in a stock. It recognizes that some shares are restricted (not available to trade, because they're owned by insiders or employees) and therefore need to be not counted in the float.

Flushing. This means what it says: it's when a stock suddenly drops in price with no warning. It may be based on news or other market circumstances.

---

[30] https://www.fa-mag.com/news/nine-years-on--the-true-story-of-the-2010-flash-crash-44742.html

Forex. Abbreviation for "foreign exchange market." This term relates to the practice of trading different currencies hoping you can make money by buying one type and selling another type. There is a lively market around forex, but I don't focus on that type of trading.

Futures. Short for "futures contracts" which relate to trading or investing in commodities. The futures contract is an agreement to buy or sell a specific commodity at a set time in the future, for a set price.

Gap. When a stock opens higher or lower than the previous day, it has gapped. It may gap up or gap down, depending on what's going on with it. Gaps are so critical to day trading that I have a custom-built gapper chart I review first thing in the morning, and pretty much continuously.

Going sideways. A market that is going sideways will fluctuate within a narrow band. For day traders it's a sign to watch and wait, and not take any action. That's because there's no telling how long it may be before some catalyst causes that stock to make a big move on big volume.

Green day. You made more money trading today than you started out with. The same concept applies to green weeks, months, and so on.

Guardrails. This is not an industry term, but it's my term to describe the principles and constraints I followed—or wish I had—when trading. Guardrails help to keep emotions in check and lessen (but not eliminate) risks.

HFT. High-Frequency Trading. These are the biggest banks, hedge funds, and other specialists who create programs and systems to trade literally in millionths of a second. A very large percentage of all stock trades are done by computers this way.

Halts. Also called trading halts or stock halts. These are brief suspensions of trading in a particular stock, usually because there is some potentially big news or event. It could be a regulatory development, or some transaction like a secondary offering, or even because of a 10 percent or greater change in the price within a five-minute period.

Halts give people a chance to digest whatever news or event happened. They rarely last more than an hour, but occasionally do.

IPO. Initial Public Offering. This is when a company "goes public" by issuing its first publicly traded shares.

Index. A portfolio that's a calculated representation of a market as a whole, or a sector, or some other slice. For example, the S&P 500 and Dow Jones Industrial Average are the most-famous indices, and they reflect different aspects of the stock market. They are benchmarks that provide a way to compare performance over time, or performance between different dimensions of the market, like tech stocks. You can day trade index funds, but it's uncommon, because they don't move that much in a day.

Level 2. Most people who've glanced at stock-market quotes are familiar with seeing the bid and asked prices. That's known as Level 1. When you have access to Level 2—which you do need as a day trader—you get to see much more detail. Not only do you see various exchanges that currently show quotes for a stock, but also what their specific quotes are, and for how many shares.

Limit order. This is an order type or instruction to your broker. A limit order indicates that you want to buy or sell a security at a specific price, or better. If you have a buy limit order for $10, then that means you want the broker to buy the stock when the price drops to $10 or below. A sell limit order of $8 means you want to automatically sell when the stock hits $8 or higher. Keep in mind that an instruction is not a guarantee. In fast-moving markets, those instructions may not happen as planned: if you want to buy at $10.00, there may not be a seller who likes the price of $10.00 and you might get some or all of your order filled at $10.15.

Liquidity. It refers to how quickly a stock can be traded without affecting its price. If you're selling 1,000 shares of Tesla, that might seem like a lot, but it will not change the price of Tesla. However, if you do the same for a small-cap stock that rarely sees much trading volume, that single order may affect the stock price.

Margin. This is the money that is borrowed from a brokerage company to buy stock. There are detailed rules about how much a trader or investor can borrow, and how it must be paid back. In some cases, the brokerage company can force the sale of stock to "cover" or pay back that margin.

Margin call. This is a demand by a broker that the trader put up more money as collateral, because of changes in the stock price. The broker wants to protect the loan it made to the trader.

Market cap. Market capitalization. If you take all outstanding shares, and multiply them by the current price, you get the market cap. If that number is more than $10 billion, it's called a large-cap stock. If it's from $2 billion to $10 billion, then it's a mid-cap. And if it's between $300 million and less than $2 billion, it's a small-cap stock. Stocks below $300 million are known as micro-cap. Companies under $50 million are nano-caps.

I stay away from large caps (and usually mid-cap stocks) because there is a ton of programmed trading in them. They are really tough to read because of the rules and triggers that computerized trading firms build into their algorithms. It's *possible* to day trade them if there is some big news happening; Tesla is a good example. It has a cult following and on any day, no one knows what Elon Musk will tweet. Even so, I tend to do better with small caps.

Market makers. These are traders who profit by providing liquidity to the rest of the market. They usually hold an inventory of shares in a stock, and will provide a bid and ask price for that stock. This is in contrast with exchanges, which provide bid and ask prices, but do not hold shares for their own account. Exchanges do work closely with market makers, however.

MOMO. This refers to momentum in the market for a stock. By momentum, we mean the level of aggressiveness in the market. If there is strong positive momentum, then traders climb over each other to buy the stock. Momentum can also be in the negative direction. Even in things as abstract as financial markets, there is such a thing as waves washing over the stocks.

OTC. Over The Counter. It is also known as OTC Pink. This is a stock market composed of broker-dealers that are electronically connected, and who trade stocks outside of an exchange. These stocks tend to be low-priced "penny stocks," and usually are priced under $5 and sometimes cost just a few cents per share. The original listings of these stocks were printed on long, skinny pink sheets; hence the OTC Pink name. I don't often trade penny stocks because they're thinly traded and there is not as much information available about them.

Options. They are not stocks, but are securities based on stocks. They allow you to buy and sell the underlying asset at certain prices, and options expire on a specified date. Options can be tempting to trade, but they are best avoided by beginners, who are much more likely to lose money than make money from them.

PDT. Pattern Day Trader. According to regulators, you are a "pattern day trader" if you execute four or more "day trades" in five business days or less. Your broker keeps track of such things and if you meet the definition, you must maintain at least $25,000 in your account and it must be a margin account. It's legal to day trade in an offshore account with as little as $500.

Penny stock. Officially a stock whose cost per share is less than $5 is considered a penny stock. I only call something a penny stock when it meets the traditional definition and is trading below $1.00 a share.

Program trading. This is similar to high-frequency trading in that computers are programmed to execute trades on specific stocks or portfolios of stocks. However, the emphasis on high-frequency trading is on how quickly the trades can be executed. Both program trading and HFT are important for day traders to be aware of, because they can affect the patterns we see when a stock trades.

Red day. You lost money trading today. Or you could have a red week, month, or any other period.

Resistance. This is a level where a stock seems to have a ceiling; it appears to stop short of the level and fall back down. Except sometimes stocks will have a breakthrough to some other resistance level. Resistance is the opposite of "support."

Revenge trading. This is a form of emotional hijacking. First a trader experiences a loss; the trader then tries to make up for the loss by taking increasingly risky trades.

Reversal. If the S&P 500 has been rallying for months, and traders spot a signal that a sell-off is coming, they are aiming to profit from the reversal of that bull trend. At the end of an uptrend, you typically see a loss of steam and volume, as well as lower highs before the market settles into a tight range. It's commonly after the downside break of this range that we see the actual "reversal" that many traders look for.

Round lot. When you buy or sell 100 shares, that is a round lot.

S&P 500. Short for Standard & Poor's 500. This is a stock-market index of 500 large-cap companies in the US. It is considered to be a proxy or reflection of the stock market, even though many other indices exist.

Scaling. As in "scaling in" and "scaling out." Entering or exiting a position gradually instead of all at once. Day traders use this as a method of reducing risk. It enables them to avoid trying to time the "perfect moment" to get in or out of a position.

Secondary offering. The sale of additional shares, after a company has had an IPO or Initial Public Offering. Though the company received proceeds from the IPO, it will not get proceeds from the secondary offering. That is because the existing shareholders' ownership in the company is being diluted by the secondary offering, so the existing shareholders will receive those proceeds.

Setup. This refers to a particular pattern of candlesticks that a stock exhibits. Based on prior experience, this pattern gives traders a clue about possible future behavior of the stock. Setups come in a great many configurations.

Shares outstanding. It is the sum of all shares currently held by all shareholders, even if some of those shares are restricted from being traded. It is to be distinguished from "float" which refers to shares that are technically available to trade.

Short Sale Restriction. This is also known as "SSR." It means that you can only short a stock on an uptick, or rise in the price. SSR is turned on when a stock drops over 10 percent in price versus the previous day's close. It was put in place to prevent a cascade of people (or computers) shorting a stock as it is going down, and therefore driving it further down by their short sales.

Short selling. Also known as shorting or being short. This is when you borrow shares from a broker in a margin account, and then sell them. You hope that the stock price will go down, at which point you will buy them. Your profit will be the difference (after fees) between the sales and purchase price, even though you did so in reverse order. Not all stocks can be shorted, because it requires your broker to have the shares available for you to borrow. If it has too-small of an inventory for what you want to do, you won't be able to short the stock through that broker.

Short squeeze. This is one downside of being a short seller. You "short" or sell a stock, hoping that it will drop in price and you can buy it lower. Instead, the stock goes higher. This is a dangerous position for short sellers to be in. If the stock continues to go higher, those short sellers will be forced by their brokers to execute buy orders. That action drives the stock even higher and is known as a short squeeze.

Slippage. This refers to the difference between the price that you expect a trade to happen at, and the actual price. It usually happens in more-volatile markets.

Spread. The difference between the bid and ask prices. For stocks that have lots of trading volume, the spread can be one penny or less. For thinly traded stocks, it can be many dollars.

Stock market sectors. These are areas of the stock market like energy, healthcare, real estate, and others. I trade mainly tech stocks, with occasional ones in retail, financial, pharmaceutical, or shipping stocks. In these sectors, I trade almost always on the small-cap side, because they're more likely to make a big move. It's not a bad idea to become familiar with one or more sectors and their trading patterns, so you can act quickly when news happens in that sector.

Stop price. Also known as a stop or stop loss. This is like a trigger to buy or sell a stock when a stock reaches this price. If that happens, the price triggers a market order for the stock. Keep in mind that if the market is volatile, just because the stop price was activated, it does not guarantee that the stock was bought or sold at that price.

Support. This is a perceived floor in prices, such that the stock regularly may approach this level but does not go below it. Demand is strong enough for the stock that when it reaches this level, traders buy it. Sometimes the support level is broken, and the stock trades down to some other, new support level. Support is the opposite of "resistance."

Technical breakout. This refers to what a stock exhibits in terms of price, independent of any news about the stock. When it is a technical breakout, the stock breaks through the usual support or resistance levels, and creates new levels.

Technical indicators. Refers to data points, ratios, and other metrics that help day traders to predict what might happen next. They include measures like a Relative Strength Index, and various volume indicators.

Thick market. This is the opposite of a thin market, and it's where there are many buyers and sellers. It's a congested situation, and sometimes is called a "stacked Level 2" or a "crowded stock."

Thin market. Also called narrow market, it's where there are few buyers and sellers. It often involves large spreads between bid and ask prices, and high price volatility. It's not a great market for day traders.

Uptick. If a stock upticks, it goes higher in price than the last transaction.

VIX. This stands for the Chicago Board Options Exchange Volatility Index. It attempts to represent the stock market's expectations for volatility over the next thirty days.

Volatility. This term refers to the magnitude of swings in the price of a stock in a period. There are a variety of ways to measure it, and it can move in either an upward or downward direction. Volatility can refer to both the market at large, and also to a specific stock.

CHAPTER 16

List of Guardrails

#1: (Chapter 2): This is my stock scanning system for momentum day trading: I focus on stocks with the following characteristics:

1. Up over 10 percent on the day versus the previous day's closing price.
2. High relative volume (at least 2.0)
3. Share prices are between $2 and $10, and not more than $20.
4. News or some other catalyst is announced today.
5. Lower floats and therefore greater volatility (preferably twenty million shares or fewer).

#2: (Chapter 5): I should have used a simulator and proven that I could be profitable before ever risking a dime of real money.

#3: (Chapter 6): In retrospect, I would not trade on margin until I've proven that I can make money consistently using my own cash.

#4: (Chapter 6): I would have avoided shorting stocks with real money until I established a profitable track record of trading in a simulator for at least 3-6 months.

#5: (Chapter 8): I generally look for trades with a minimum 2:1 profit/loss ratio.

#6: (Chapter 8): It's crucial—but not enough—for me to know my profit/loss ratio on a trade. I work hard to stick to those boundaries in the heat of trading. Changing risk parameters to accommodate a bad trade has not worked well in my experience.

#7: (Chapter 8): To maximize my ability to make the right decisions under stress, I try to exercise and meditate every day. It's one of the best ways to keep my discipline muscle strong.

#8: (Chapter 8): I set *and follow* a maximum loss amount per trade, and a maximum loss amount per day.

#9: (Chapter 8): Sometimes I ask my broker to set a max position size (both in shares and dollar value), and a max daily loss on my account.

#10: (Chapter 8): I never want to have one trade weighted so heavily with risk that it has the power to erase more than one or two previous winners.

#11: (Chapter 8): I trade the market I'm in, not the market I want to be in. I throttle up when it's hot, throttle down when it's cold, and do everything possible to minimize drawdown so that each day I come to the table confident and ready to perform at my best.

#12: (Chapter 10): I've found that trading the right stock is much more important than trading the right pattern.

#13: (Chapter 10): Each day when I sit down and am looking at potential stocks to trade, I ask myself: *Is this the strongest stock today?*

#14: (Chapter 10): My goal each day is to pull ten to fifteen cents per share out of the market.

#15: (Chapter 10): I look not only for the strongest stock today but I also ask myself, *Is this the obvious one?*

#16: (Chapter 11): In retrospect, my goal should have been that I would be ready to trade when I had proven that I was ready; not when I merely thought it was time.

#17: (Chapter 11): I keep a trading journal, and update it after each trading day.

#18: (Chapter 11): I regularly analyze my journal for clues about the conditions that generate green and red days for me. When I'm in a slump, I study my journal even more.

#19: (Chapter 11): In retrospect, I've realized that I could have saved a lot of effort and money by resisting the temptation to blaze a new trail. When I'm learning something new, I now follow what the professionals do as much as I possibly can.

#20: (Chapter 11): When starting out, I should have made just one trade per day until I could show five or six green weeks in a row.

Acknowledgments

There are a number of people whose efforts contributed to the publication of this book, and I'd like to acknowledge them. This book would not have been possible without the support of Jonathan Rozek. About a year ago, I received a letter from a big New York publisher, who wanted me to sign a two-book deal. I put off responding to them for a few months, not because I was playing hard to get but because the prospect of writing a new book was overwhelming.

When I wrote my first book in 2015, I was living alone. I had no children, and I had a lot more time to focus than I do now. But I had been thinking about a new book and this was the catalyst I needed to get me started. The publisher recommended calling Jon and speaking to him about my project. He's a terrific writer with extensive knowledge of the financial markets. They thought he might be the perfect person to help me organize my ideas for a new book, and they were right.

I'd also like to extend a thank you to the members of my team who work behind the scenes to make everything feel seamless for our members at Warrior Trading. They allowed me to have the space I needed to work on this book. They also proofread early drafts and gave honest feedback.

And last, but certainly not least, I have to extend a debt of gratitude to my wife and two boys, who experienced the sacrifice of me tucked away in my office while I focused on writing this new book for all of the aspiring traders out there.

Index

The Journey Continues!

Thanks for getting and reading my book.

If you want to continue learning about how to day trade,
I have something for you.

I created a free mini series of videos that is an extension of this book.
This series focuses specifically on the material you'll need to learn
and the skills you'll want to refine in order to start trading with
confidence and conviction. These are the next steps in your journey.

Currently this video series is only available for readers of this book.

The videos are my gift to you, to support you in your journey to
becoming a day trader. You can get them by going to:
www.warriortrading.com/bookbonus

Made in United States
Troutdale, OR
02/26/2024